The Handbook of

Chinese Snuff Bottles

Trevor W. Cornforth and Dr. Nathan Cheung

Schiffer Publishing Ltd

4880 Lower Valley Road, Atglen, PA 19310 USA

Library of Congress Cataloging-in-Publication Data

Comforth, Trevor W.
The handbook of Chinese snuff bottles / Trevor W. Comforth, Nathan Cheung.
p. cm.
ISBN 0-7643-1590-0
1. Snuff boxes and bottles--China. 2. Snuff boxes and bottles--Collectors and collecting. I. Cheung, Nathan. II. Title.
NK9507 .C68 2002
745.593'4'0951075--dc21
2002002140

Photography by Trevor Cornforth

Designed by Bonnie M. Hensley
Cover design by Bruce M. Waters
Type set in BauerBodni BdCn BT/Lydian BT

ISBN: 0-7643-1590-0
Printed in China
1 2 3 4

Published by Schiffer Publishing Ltd.
4880 Lower Valley Road
Atglen, PA 19310
Phone: (610) 593-1777; Fax: (610) 593-2002
E-mail: Schifferbk@aol.com
Please visit our web site catalog at www.schifferbooks.com
We are always looking for people to write books on new and related subjects.
If you have an idea for a book please contact us at the above address.

This book may be purchased from the publisher. Include $3.95 for shipping. Please try your bookstore first. You may write for a free catalog.

In Europe, Schiffer books are distributed by
Bushwood Books
6 Marksbury Ave.
Kew Gardens
Surrey TW9 4JF England
Phone: 44 (0) 20 8392-8585; Fax: 44 (0) 20 8392-9876
E-mail: Bushwd@aol.com
Free postage in the U.K., Europe; air mail at cost.

Contents

Acknowledgments _____ 4
Introduction _____ 5
    What Are The Prices Of Snuff Bottles? _____ 7
1. History and Development of Snuffing _____ 9
2. Chinese Symbolism & Decoration _____ 12
3. Stone Snuff Bottles _____ 21
4. Glass Snuff Bottles _____ 47
5. Enameled Snuff Bottles _____ 79
6. Porcelain Snuff Bottles _____ 86
7. A Hotchpotch of Other Materials _____ 109
8. Inside Painted Snuff Bottles _____ 127
9. Fakes & Forgeries _____ 156
10. Care & Display _____ 159
Bibliography _____ 160

Acknowledgments

The writing of this book would not have been possible without the help of several individuals. We would like to thank Jo and Brian Penny, Zvi and Angela Klemer, Yan Dongmei (China Guardian Auctions Company Ltd., Beijing), Chen Xia, Matthew and Caroline Skippen, for loaning us their beautiful collections. We are also extremely grateful to Aixinjueluo (Aisingioro) Yu Lan, Li Zengming, Jin Yu and Yan Guiping in Beijing, for permission to include some of their snuff bottles in this book. We also thank Ma Jun for his photography of the snuff bottles from these Chinese collectors based in Beijing.

We have, for each illustrated bottle, named the owner of the piece where appropriate. However, should there be one or two bottles without the name of their owners, we sincerely apologize to the respective collector.

Before even writing the book, we must say thank you to Judy Smith for getting the ball rolling, Bob Marion for his delightful illustration, Nik Ragg for his photographic advice and Zhu Cui Ying (Adams) for her invaluable translation.

Tintin Zheng comes last but far from least for his invaluable help in China.

Introduction

One of the first things you would expect to see in any book on Chinese antiques is a complex dynastic table that chronicles the last three thousand years of China's civilized history. This extended period of civilization, arguably longer than any other in the world, has seen the unification of a vast nation of diverse cultures, the development of political structure and government, the growth of education and art, record keeping and accounting and countless other aspects which make China unique.

Despite all of this, you will find here only the tables which chronicle Chinese rulers of the last three hundred and fifty years or so, since the arrival, from the north, of the Qing dynasty (pronounced Ching) in 1644. Historically known as the last dynasty it began after the ousting of the last Ming Emperor Chongzhen, and lasted until 1912 when its own last Emperor, Xuantong (Aisingioro Pu Yi) was ousted by the people.

References to Imperial names will be in the modern idiom based upon Pinyin, the phonetic Mandarin of the late twentieth century, and not the earlier and more complex spellings. This may confuse the collector who reads more widely since some books use earlier spellings and others use the personal rather than post enthronement names.

Last imperial dynasty it may have been but in modern China, certainly in antique dealing circles, you will often hear the phrase or expression Mao Dy or Mao dynasty. Had it not been for political upheaval and discrediting of Chairman Mao's widow, it could well have been exactly that with each successor related to or chosen by the former premier. The reason for concentrating solely on the period since 1644 is that snuff bottles are a relatively recent addition to the Chinese culture and only really became popular in the eighteenth and nineteenth centuries.

This book differs from others, particularly those on snuff bottles, in that it doesn't end with the last Emperor but continues right up to the present day.

Later bottles are usually referred to disparagingly as "made for tourists," since the habit of taking snuff had largely died out by the end of the nineteenth century, but this ignores the charm and merits of the later pieces and seeks to keep to an exclusive few, who can afford the earlier ones, the immense pleasure derived from collecting them.

There are numerous learned volumes, to which we are indebted for much of our own knowledge, which detail at length the history and development of the snuff taking culture and the subsequent development of its Chinese containers. This book will seek to cover much the same ground in a concise form but also to expand upon it based upon direct research in China and following the development of bottles beyond the end of the Qing dynasty to the present day.

We are also indebted to numerous people for their cooperation and contributions including two members of the former Imperial family who loaned bottles as examples. However, where previous books have concentrated on the rather rarefied examples on show in museums around the world, we have sought to use bottles which have changed hands in recent years so that the values given here for the first time are realistic.

The majority of early bottles have passed through one or other auction house in China, Hong Kong or Taiwan or have been handled by us in the course of business.

It is a rather typical and arrogant assumption on the part of many people that the high prices achieved for the most prized examples are because they are sold in the West. For this reason we have referred to auction values achieved in the East, where collectors are increasingly enthusiastic and also increasingly able to pay high prices, as well as typical prices asked in the West. With modern travel and Internet access it could be argued that although the auctions are in the East the buyers are Western-ers, but we are assured that is not always the case. What is also significant in relation to the principles of this book is that local Chinese collectors recognize the value, quality and skill involved in the twentieth century bottles which we have included. With inside painted bottles in particular the quality achieved today far exceeds that available in most of the nineteenth century examples.

The skill and artistry needed to produce each kind of bottle have been passed from generation to generation and from master to student and instead of being diluted with time have become more profound and expressive.

Yes, many pieces are direct copies, or reproductions, of their eighteenth or nineteenth century inspiration but have taken no less skill to produce and it is only in the West that "reproduction" or "repro" is a dirty word. The Chinese have, from dynasty to dynasty, repeatedly copied their predecessors in acknowledgment of their artistry not, as may be assumed, to make a fast buck on a fake. In China it is known as a "nod to the past", a real compliment to long dead masters from whom they can learn and a challenge to the skills of present day craftsmen. It is only with the escalating prices of original pieces that the question of faking rather than simply imitating comes into play. Interestingly, one of the twentieth century's most recognized snuff bottle creators, *Ye Bengqi*, was so good that it was not until he identified some bottles in a museum as his own work that they were regarded as anything other than eighteenth century in origin. It had merely been his intention to imitate not to fake for the sake of deception.

We shall probably have little to offer the subject scholar except perhaps a catalogue of recently achieved prices but we hope to give the new collector some insight, without too much deep study, and the inspiration to collect these delightful objects. As the title suggests it is perfectly possible to have an extensive and varied collection, including some quite early examples, without breaking the bank. As with so many other aspects of collecting the principle should be that if you see a piece that you like, the price seems reasonable and you can afford it, then buy it.

From here on in the chapters seek to answer common questions asked by buyers, particularly new ones, which often remain unanswered by inexperienced sellers and some other questions you may not have thought to ask. We have illustrated the text as much as possible and used those illustrations to locate many of the answers instead of in lengthy paragraphs and chapters. An extensive Bibliography is featured so that anyone wishing to do so may explore further.

What Are The Prices Of Snuff Bottles?

Given that one of the principle differences between this and previous books on the subject is the inclusion of a price guide, it is important for the reader to understand how these figures have been reached. The majority of snuff bottles are between 2.5" (6.5cms) and 3.5" (9cms) in height, excluding the stopper, and where the illustrated bottles fall between or very close to those sizes it has not been detailed. However, for larger or smaller bottles measurements have been added.

Many similar guides on other subjects are nothing more nor less than a printed justification of the prices being asked by the author. There is nothing inherently wrong with this provided that the basis is stated in the text.

We have set about producing a price guide based upon achieved and experienced prices both in the auction and general resale markets. On this basis a bottle that has been sold in auction will be given a fixed price, for example (A) £1,000. Another piece offered in auction but which failed to sell for whatever reason, or has not actually come up for sale at the time of writing, will be shown as, for example, (A) £1,000-£1,500 to indicate the auctioneer's guide price. Descriptions used for "auction" bottles are precisely as they appeared in the relevant catalogue.

Where a bottle is shown with a guide price, for example, £1,000-£1,500 but no (A), this indicates a range which might be expected within either the U. K. or Chinese Markets in a shop, collector's fair or market situation. In our experience prices asked in the Far East frequently exceed those achieved in the West and may require persistent negotiation before an acceptable level is achieved.

It is often assumed by collectors and dealers that this is sheer optimism and bravado on the part of the Far Eastern dealer, who assumes that those waving Sterling or U. S. dollars have unlimited bank accounts and little experience. In some cases this may be true but in general it shows that we are not their only market and that others with more money and perhaps greater appreciation will come along and purchase.

For about five years now *Trevor* has been trying to buy one particular bottle by a well-known contemporary inside bottle painter. His work is superb, rather resembling an Italian painting in the Cistine Chapel in Rome, admirable if it were on a canvas or the outside of a bottle but totally remarkable being on the inside.

Initially, the bottle was beyond a palatable price range but with greater experience and having bought and resold a bottle by the same artist, interest grew to the level of determination. However, with each return visit the price grew and yet the bottle remained unsold. No amount of argument that a price quoted on the last visit was lower would achieve the desired result and slowly its price rose and rose. Apparently it is his last bottle. He has now lost the quality of sight necessary to paint further so the selling agents have grown ambitious or in less polite terms greedy. The bottle, beautiful as it is, remains on the same shelf that it has occupied for the last five years or more.

Incidentally, the other bottle referred to above changed hands three times in one weekend and each time its price was doubled and achieved. For the best pieces, even modern, it's a strong market.

Returning to the subject of pricing within this book it is important for the reader and collector to realize that there are no set prices for any of these lovely objects. Unlike factory produced collectibles, which may bear a well known name but are produced identically in their thousands, snuff bottles are almost invariably the product of small workshops and studios and are individually crafted. As such they are generally unrepeatable even though the subject may be one used by several artists.

This unique nature means that even subtle differences in quality can make substantial differences to the price and it will be one dealer's or collector's opinion over another as to which is the superior piece.

While the age and authenticity of any particular bottle will also significantly affect its desirability it is not always as easy to tell as might be assumed. We have already seen that bottles by *Ye Bengqi* from the twentieth century were assumed to have been made much earlier and although of rare quality perhaps made prices greater than they should.

In these circumstances the provenance of a bottle becomes paramount. Fake pearls belonging to *Jackie Kennedy Onassis* reached a price in auction that would be unthinkable for other similar jewelry. Similarly, bottles known to have been in the possession of a member of the Imperial family will soar through the roof if they are offered for sale, especially with the mystique attached to this elite group.

To a lesser degree bottles that have a provenance establishing their lengthy existence in a private collection will achieve better prices than those simply stated as being old because of the experience of the assessor. Regrettably, the provenance that may have thus affected an auction value is not always apparent in the published results.

Interestingly in trawling through large numbers of catalogues from the Far East, Europe and the U. S., it has become clear that twentieth century bottles are already recognized marketable items in the major houses. We have deliberately included them even though made recently because their quality and unique nature demands it as well as their affordability for new collectors. It would appear then that we are not alone in our appreciation of them because there have been numerous bottles sold which were referred to simply as twentieth century, making absolutely no note as to whether that is early or late.

Undoubtedly some people will disagree with our pricing. Some will consider it too high and others too low but it is intended to represent a reasonable mean. As mentioned above, with no two pieces alike, it is difficult to make comparisons and inevitably the overheads of the seller and availability of good stock must be taken into account.

We do not intend that this should be treated as the "bible of snuff bottles values" but merely a buyers and collector's guide.

Readers should also bear in mind that there is a strong and established market in the higher priced and authenticated early bottles, a few of which appear here for interest and comparison, and we are not in any way attempting to undermine them. Perhaps some new collectors will eventually aspire to the very rarest pieces. What we would say, however, is that not all early bottles are confined to elite collections and some can still be purchased for reasonable sums, albeit they are the simpler ones.

Chapter One
History and Development of Snuffing

The history of Chinese snuff bottles began in Europe with the arrival of tobacco around the sixteenth century. This strange new substance quickly became a fashion accessory for the elite and wealthy being itself a statement of the user's monetary standing.

With journeys across the Atlantic to collect it being so risky and long and the limited quantities that could be carried along with other cargoes, it was an expensive product. Whether as smoking tobacco or ground into snuff, a fashionable habit must be properly dressed and a whole new supply industry arose around it. Like the tea which had arrived in Europe from China, it was similarly expensive so boxes were created for storage and security. In the nineteenth century as tobacco prices fell and the working classes began to use it, the range of containers grew enormously and many became novelty items.

In the late seventeenth and early eighteenth-centuries, however, fashion and elegance were the key and for snuff takers this meant carrying small-lidded boxes made of gold or silver. The ornamentation of these was frequently lavish and it must have been as much a fashion and wealth statement to brandish the boxes and offer a pinch of snuff to a guest or client, as it was a pleasure to carry it for one's own use.

Throughout Europe the royal courts were among the first to sample and become addicted to this new drug. It was, after all, not really portrayed as a recreational product but a magical potion which could cure headaches, fever and untold other ills. Being tobacco its addictive properties soon came into play and it is hard not to parallel it with the cocaine habits of many of society's rich and famous today.

The result of this royal patronage was a flood of fashion conscious users and collections of snuff boxes that now adorn the palaces and museums of the world seeking to portray our history.

Inevitably with merchant shipping between Europe and China increasing by the year some snuff users eventually found themselves the objects of scrutiny by their oriental associates. Sea captains, merchants and diplomats would have had ample opportunity to sample this new delight and many must have carried it with them across the sea.

It is impossible to credit any particular individual with the introduction of tobacco to China, especially in its powdered form, snuff. Numerous theories also abound as to why the Chinese chose bottles rather than boxes in which to store and carry their snuff.

Combining an understanding of the Chinese culture with one of historical context the solution seems quite clear. Whether it was Spanish, Portuguese or even British merchants who first introduced it is really quite irrelevant. It is what happened afterwards that is fascinating.

Curiosity would have required the Chinese to investigate and indeed sample this new phenomenon especially as its medicinal properties were part of its selling power. There may even have been a degree of sampling and merchandising on the part of these European travelers eager to have a new bartering tool for the valuable tea and porcelain they had come for.

The European habit of taking a pinch of snuff, a very imprecise amount, between the thumb and forefinger and then either sniffing it directly or placing it on the back of the opposite hand may well have disgusted the rather prim and proper Chinese of the period. Anyone who has taken or witnessed the taking of snuff will know that, in the European way, it is a messy business leaving the nostrils and any facial hair stained and dusty.

As the prevailing fashion in China was for long moustaches and also bright, often highly decorated silk robes it is not surprising that they sought to use the snuff differently. The Imperial nose could not be seen to be covered in dirty brown smutt nor the Imperial robes in a brown residue which would be hard to clean.

At the time many Chinese medicines consisted of powdered potions that were either ingested directly or added to water. Despite Chinese medicine's modern reputation for lack of precision, the doctors of the time were keen to keep dosage accurate and dispensed many of their medicines in small bottles with tight stoppers and narrow necks so that limited amounts could be dispensed at one time.

Doctors may well have been some of the first to see the potential in this new powder especially as it came with such a pedigree. The fact that it had arrived from Europe and was used by the elegant and well educated would certainly have added to its credibility.

Whether *vía* doctors, merchants, or Mandarins of the Qing court, the Emperor in Peking would have been quick to find out about this mysterious substance. Compared to smoking opium, smoking tobacco would have had little attraction but this fashionable, medicinal and ultimately addictive powder was something different.

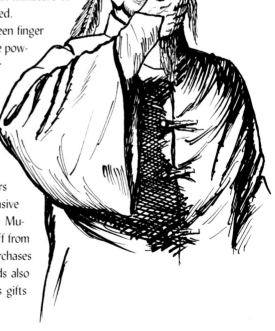

Using the same basic miniature bottles as for other medicines and a tiny spoon for transferring the powder, a new art form was born. The Chinese passion for items in miniature as well as their need for propriety were both satisfied.

Instead of the clumsy European pinch between finger and thumb, which was just not Imperial at all, the powder was taken from the bottle on a small ivory or metal spoon and transferred to the back of the thumb nail and then the nail placed carefully beneath the nostril before inhaling. The smaller quantity and greater precision would have been much cleaner and if justification were necessary it was most certainly medicinal.

Whether the Qing Emperors were avid users of snuff is hard to determine. The very extensive records of the Forbidden City (now the Palace Museum) in Peking (Beijing) show many gifts of snuff from foreign and Chinese dignitaries and numerous purchases of it for the Imperial stock. However, the records also indicate that large amounts were given away as gifts and tributes.

What we do know is that without exception the subsequent Emperors became avid collectors of snuff bottles employing craftsmen from around the world to create an ever more impressive variety. Porcelain and enamel workers were brought from *Jingdezhen* and *Canton*, ivory workers from *Suzhou*, lacquer workers from Japan and enamellers from Germany. Each was to expand the limits of their miniaturized art form to please the Emperor's voracious appetite. In addition, tributes both local and foreign frequently consisted of exotic bottles made to celebrate the Imperial birthday or one of the important annual festivals.

The Forbidden City records document tens of thousands of bottles both in and out but in the latter days of the Imperial household, especially once the last Emperor was deposed in 1911, huge numbers would have disappeared, unofficially!

In his own account of the fall of the Qing dynasty, *Aisingioro Pu Yi* (Emperor Xuantong) recalls that many items were sold in order to maintain the expenses of his huge court. Despite having been deposed, the Emperor and his household remained in the Forbidden City until 1924 and continued to receive an allowance but it was insufficient for the size of the court and the lavish lifestyle they led.

In addition to the bottles sold these small objects would have been easy to steal and many must have fallen victim to the hands of a eunuch or Palace official. Many of them maintained households of their own outside the Forbidden City walls and with significantly reduced income would have found it hard to manage.

Aisingioro Pu Yi speaks of numerous fires that occurred in the latter days clearly designed to destroy records of what might have gone missing if an investigation were launched.

The book "*Masterpieces of Snuff Bottles*" in the Palace Museum records that between two thousand and three thousand bottles remain in the collection, many of which are stored in specially designed boxes. Many more are in museums and private collections around the world but with few detailed records to go on it is difficult to date and provenance the majority.

Helen White in "*Snuff Bottles from China, The Victoria and Albert Museum Collection*" is very cautious on dating, quoting for example, c1767-1910. The earlier date indicates when the style or type was first recorded, the latter when the bottle was acquired by the collector who bequeathed it. This very broad band acknowledges that without specific recorded provenance it is impossible to be sure. In China, as in many other countries, it was normal to repeat pieces, styles and materials that had proved popular. After all, that makes common sense.

It is reasonable to conclude then that even in the most unlikely place one might just purchase a bottle that was once in the Imperial Collection but went astray. Such a bottle may well be a very simple one made of wood, jade, glass or other material because by far the majority of those made were not the lavish and precious objects one might expect. Many of those still in the Palace Museum collection would be considered simple and tactile rather than ornate and expensive.

Emperors of the Qing Dynasty (1644-1912)

Emperor	Reign	Emperor	Reign
Shunzhi (*Hsun-chih*)	1644-1661	Daoguang (*Tao-kuang*)	1821-1850
Kangxi (*K'ang-hsi*)	1662-1722	Xianfeng (*Hsien-feng*)	1851-1861
Yongzheng (*Yung-cheng*)	1723-1735	Tongzhi (*T'ung-chih*)	1862-1874
Qianlong (*Ch'ien-lung*)	1736-1795	Guangxu (*Kuang-hsu*)	1875-1908
Jiaqing (*Chia-ch'ing*)	1796-1820	Xuantong (*Hsuan-t'ung*)	1909-1911

Chapter Two
Chinese Symbolism & Decoration

The principal influences behind most Chinese art and decoration throughout its long history have been symbolism, legend and history. The symbolism relates mostly to the aspirations of its population for health, wealth and many years to enjoy them. The stories of legend and history have often been expanded and enhanced by the artistic representations they have received taking acts of magic and heroism to extremes greater than when they began.

As in art generally the decorative influences on snuff bottles follow similar lines and it will be clear when examining both actual and illustrated examples just how important they are.

The enjoyment from collecting is, therefore, greatly enhanced by an understanding of what lies behind the picture and perhaps the context in which a particular bottle may have been given. Decorative as they may be it is a shame to treat them solely at face value since they offer a tremendous insight into the Chinese culture of the recent and ancient past.

In reality with regional variations and superstitions it may be possible to extend a list of symbols to every blade of grass and animal in the country but for most people's purposes a reasonable insight will suffice. In this respect a full analysis is beyond the scope of this and most other books. A reasonable number of the most frequently encountered and most important examples will help the reader and collector.

The complexity and unusual sounds of the Chinese language have resulted in much of what we now see as symbols. The similarity of the words *fu* (meaning bat) and *fu* (meaning happiness) with their tonal variations has meant that the image of a bat is used to represent and invoke happiness. That seems straightforward enough except that it only applies in Mandarin which was and still remains mostly a language of the north and of officialdom. To most Cantonese speakers in the South it is the exact opposite and the bat is associated with bad luck and therefore unhappiness.

The list below is a guide to general symbolism with more specific details being given to accompany some of the bottles illustrated. The list is endless, but it is already clear that the associations are repetitive. Add to this clouds, water (both rippled and still), sacks of grain, ancient coins, mountains, waterfalls and many more and you have the stimuli for the artist's imagination and also the means by which he can sell his work.

The Yin and Yang Symbol

Representing positive and negative, female and male and ultimately the dualism of the universe this is very much a sign related to balance. It is regularly associated in modern terms with the art of *Feng Shui* and the balances of life brought about through Buddhism.

The Eighteen *Lohan*

These rather colorful characters, the personal disciples of Buddha, have each been credited with supernatural powers. Depicted singly or as a group they are frequently seen in Chinese art and are associated overall with spiritual and supernatural influence for the recipient.

The Eight Immortals

These equally or even more colorful characters, probably more easily recognized in the West, are rooted in Taoism and are the Taoist equivalent of the *Lohan*. They are more specifically separated in their symbolic roles with poverty, wealth, aristocracy, common birth, age, youth, masculinity and femininity.

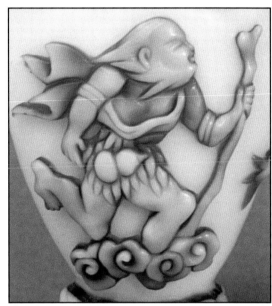

Probably best known of these is *Shou Lao*, more correctly referred to as *Lao Shou Xing*, since *Lao* means old and *Shou Xing* is his nickname (real name *Zhang Guo Lao*), whose extra large head associates him not only with age but also wisdom and experience. He is particularly evidential of the Chinese reverence for old age that has resulted in many wonderful images of gnarled elderly women and men in both painted and carved form.

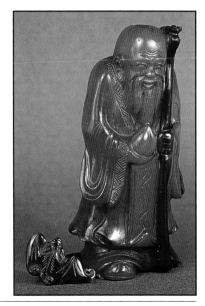

The Eight Taoist Emblems

These include the fan, sword, gourd, castanets, flower basket, bamboo rods or drum, flute and lotus.

The Eight Buddhist Emblems

These include the wheel or bell, conch, umbrella, canopy, lotus, vase, pair of fish, endless knots of entrails.

The One Hundred Children

A very popular image is known as the One Hundred Children though there is little point in counting them since they are rarely shown in their entirety. Numbers may vary from twenty or so upwards but are nonetheless recognized as the necessary hundred. It may seem excessive but they are associated with the desire for fertility and would often be given as part of a wedding or anniversary gift.

The Chinese Lion Dogs

Chinese lion dogs (known as *Fo* or *Fu*) are usually shown in pairs. One represents the male and the other the female. The male dog has a ball (known as a *chu*) in its mouth which represents his life essence. The ball is sometimes represented as a composite of several old coins or "cash" by which it is assumed he is intended to guard the owner's wealth. The female dog is usually protecting a cub and is an emblem of bravery, energy and strength.

The Dragon

The dragon is the symbol of the Emperor and is associated with strength, goodness, vigilance, protection and power. Chinese dragons are subdivided into sky, earth, water and mountain dragons.

They are represented with three, four or five toes, the latter being more auspicious. Legends involving dragons mean that several are sometimes seen entwined, they may be holding a pearl or playing with balls of fire and in their stylized form they can often be mistaken for a lesser creature such as a tiger or panther.

To a Chinese dealer, an item decorated with a five-toed dragon is automatically worth more than any other one with fewer toes.

The Phoenix

Symbol of the Empress it may be seen in mirror image, singly or opposite the dragon. Also sometimes stylized almost beyond recognition it represents the sun, warmth, summer and harvest.

The Unicorn

Unlike the Western image of a horse with a single horn on its forehead the Chinese unicorn is truly a creature of myth. Most often depicted as a mixture of other animals gone awry it is a wonder to behold but little used for artistic representation, certainly on snuff bottles. It is symbolic of longevity, wisdom and grandeur.

The Tortoise

Perhaps because of its slow pace and generally long life the Chinese and Hindus both use it to represent the universe. Associated with longevity, strength and endurance it is often depicted with a crane or other creature standing on its back as in many Chinese memorials.

The Year Signs

The twelve cyclic year signs all have their share of representation on snuff bottles. All would have been obvious gifts for birthdays some having additional symbolism and significance.

The monkey is an emblem of guile and trickery though he is venerated in Buddhism. The ox symbolizes spring and agriculture as well as the obvious association with hard work and strength. The horse claims speed, perseverance, power and wealth.

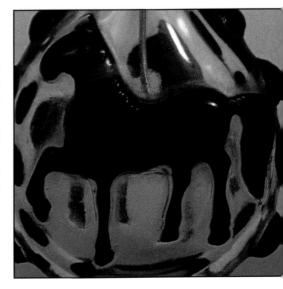

The tiger was considered to be the emblem of nobility below the Emperor and so is an important figure seen on many works of art for the aristocracy. The tiger represents the male force or Yang, and symbolizes dignity, sternness and bravery. The hare, balancing the tiger, is the Yin or female force and is said to enhance longevity.

While the other seven must not be ignored, their symbolism may be considered less important, except to those whose birth makes them an influential factor.

The Deer, Crane, and Stork
Each is a symbol of longevity and not, as might be assumed in the latter case, babies. Western dealers frequently make the mistake of assuming an association which they suggest would mean a blessing of babies and therefore a link with marriage and fertility.

The Bear

Though little used the bear would be associated with bravery and strength.

The Elephant

Also associated with strength the elephant has wisdom, prudence and power on his side. The word *xiang* meaning elephant has the same basic sound as *xiang* meaning auspicious, hence the use of elephant decoration for special occassions.

Chan – The Three Legged Toad

Based on a legend of a creature spitting money he is an obvious symbol of wealth. The pronunciation of *Chan* or *Chen* is also similar to *Qian* meaning money.

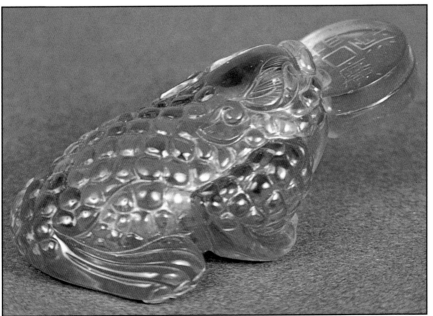

The Bat

Already mentioned in the introduction to the chapter, the bat generally symbolizes happiness.

The Cicada

This noisy summer insect is seen as the epitome of reincarnation and immortality.

The Squirrel and Grapes

Both individually and together these two symbolize longevity.

The Fish

Wealth and abundance are transformed to harmony and union when the fish is doubled to two, though unlike the symbol Pisces where the fish swim in opposite directions, the Chinese version swim together.

The Lotus

Growing year-in and year-out from the stench of the mud at the bottom of a stagnant pond, the lotus, and in particular its flower, is a symbol of purity. The bud, blossom, and seed-pod represent the past, present, and future.

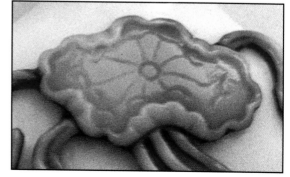

The Bamboo

Bamboo is often used to represent an individual who is upright and respectable though its general symbolism is more closely associated with longevity due to the bamboo's durability.

The Peach

Frequently depicted in the hand of the Taoist Immortal *Shou Lao* opposite the knotty staff in his other hand, the peach adds immortality and longevity to his attributes. The peach's soft texture and color and luxurious flesh is also associated with birthdays.

The Gourd

This fruit brings together fertility and longevity.

Chapter Three
Stone Snuff Bottles

Arguably the most tactile of the numerous types available, stone bottles offer endless variety. This variety leads to difficulties of identification when trying to define stones as clearly as possible since not all experts will agree. Still more confusing is the fact that most international auction houses fail to fully define them and group all jade-like stones together as jade and many others simply as rock crystal. While we have tried to be as precise as possible some collectors may disagree with our choices.

Most popular among Chinese collectors was and still is jade. While in the West many specialists differentiate between jade, jadeite, chalcedony and so on the Chinese tend to group these together often also including pale agates. They are all technically different stones and yet in *Jade* (*Anness Publishing Limited, 1991*) they are defined collectively under that general jade heading. Taking the word *Yu* in Chinese, which simply means a stone which can be carved, broadens the definition of Jade beyond the basic Jadeite and Nephrite. This, however, is creating difficulties of definition beyond the scope of anything less than an encyclopedic volume and so would be inappropriate here.

Whichever way the materials are defined it is usually the subtlety of design and decoration which makes this group of bottles so popular and often so expensive. The artist's undoubted foresight in carving and polishing a bottle to such a precise shape or style of decoration that the natural colors are enhanced is remarkable and indeed it is this particular feature which is so sought after.

Two dark spots in an otherwise plain piece of stone will create the eyes of a fish. A slight flick in the tail may be carved to take advantage of a few natural streaks which in turn enhance the appeal of a tail fin.

Such fine and subtle details have been the delight of generations of emperors and snuff bottle collectors. The hollowing of the bottles until they are translucent and in some cases only one or two millimeters thick is a major feat in itself with flaws and layers in the stones always threatening fragmentation. Neck and foot details and often carved lion heads and ring decoration on the shoulders simply add to the complexity of the work and the enjoyment of the end product.

Several complex figure subjects are illustrated where the carver or polisher has used hats or other details to disguise the presence of the stopper. In more conventional shaped bottles it is a distinct advantage to have the original stopper designed for the bottle because these are usually of the same material and often exhibit the same color details as the main body. In other types of bottles it may be impossible and really irrelevant to know whether the stopper is original. Many glass bottles were made with stone, coral, silver or gold tops but few stone bottles appear to have been made with contrasting stoppers.

We generally refer to the method of decoration as carving. This wrongly implies some sort of whittling process involving a blade. In many inland areas of China, particularly those close to the material sources, fine "carving" still goes on and it may be possible to watch the artist at work. The modern craftsman is helped by electricity but uses the same basic tools as have been worked for generations. Being much harder than the cameo glass, mentioned in the chapter on glass, and with many natural flaws leading to fragmentation, the stone whether it is jade or agate is difficult to work.

The cutting tool is a little like a drill bit though with a ball like end of varying size and coarseness to create the fine or larger detail and polishing. The cutting or drilling tool is in a fixed place, though the angle may be variable, and it is the material being worked which is moved to and from the rapidly spinning bit.

In the not too distant past, even late into the twentieth century, many workshops used treadle like machines, similar to old sewing machines, with the artist using his foot to propel the tool. This metal version was an extension and development of the "pole lathe" used in both East and West for centuries to decorate wood and other materials. In that instance the wood was turned and the blade held to it but the basic principle of operating the tool was much the same.

It is only when one has seen a craftsman begin work on a solid lump of stone with no drawing or plan in front of him that the miracle of the end product is understood. Some time ago in China one particular carver explained that if he was working on a really special piece of stone, he meditated on it. This he said allowed him to know the stone and really understand what was inside in terms of color and strata. Once he had done that he felt that he and the stone knew each other and could work together to produce a suitable end product. As he began on this hard lump of rock he "knew" what he was going to create and where to find the details of color to really make it come alive. Seeing his work in progress a few days later I realized that was exactly what he was doing as detail after detail began to emerge naturally from the stone as if it were there all the time and just waiting for him to reveal it.

It is workmanship such as this and devotion to detail which makes a serious group of collectors look for nothing other than Chinese artifacts whether they are snuff bottles or other products.

As with other sections we have left the bottles to speak for themselves enhancing them, where possible with explanations and descriptions. With stone bottles, more than any other material, there is no substitute for holding them, caressing them in the fingers and trying to get inside the mind of the creator be that Divine or artistic.

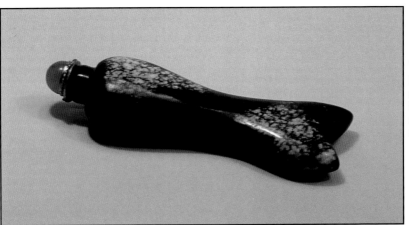

The mottled areas of this dark chalcedony quartz highlight the image of its fish shaped carving. £50-60. $70-85

The proud shape of this bulbous bottle on a tall foot beautifully sets off the exotic color of this goldstone bottle. Its matching stopper enhances the overall appearance. £60-80. $85-115

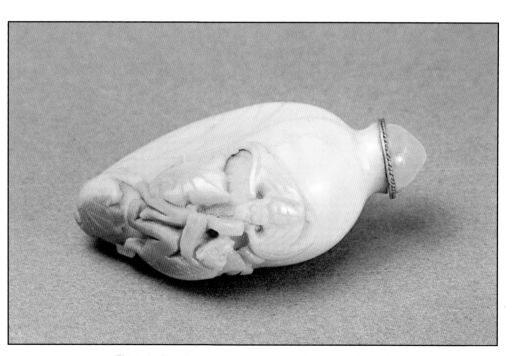

This jade-like pale green and brown pebble has been enhanced by the carving of a monkey and a bat. £50-60. $70-85

A piece of very impure jade has been chosen for this rather crudely carved bottle depicting a mouse on a rock. Despite its simplicity this is an attractive bottle and is probably around one hundred years old. £60-80. $85-115

The mottled light colored areas highlight this dark chalcedony bottle. £40-50. $55-70

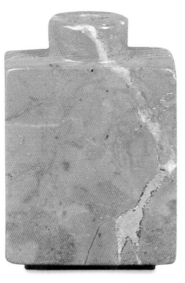

A very simple box-like red stone bottle which resembles a Cantonese tea caddy. £30-40. $40-55

The colored strata in this pebble have been carved to best advantage and show a bat which has landed on a vine with gourds. The carving is crude but the overall effect pleasing. £60-80. $85-115

A small obsidian cicada is the delightful result of this carver's work. It is unclear what form the original stopper would have taken but it may have been or resembled a black pearl. *Courtesy of Penny Collection.* £80-100. $115-145

Two small carved turquoise bottles of slightly different color. The dark inclusions would make this stone unsuitable for jewelry but enhance its use here. £120-150 each. $175-215

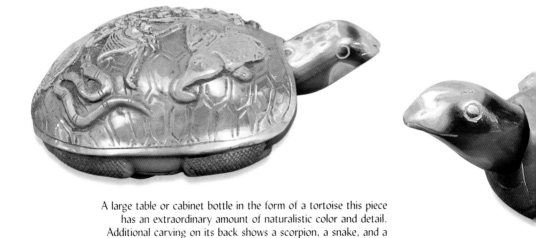

A large table or cabinet bottle in the form of a tortoise this piece has an extraordinary amount of naturalistic color and detail. Additional carving on its back shows a scorpion, a snake, and a frog. The head removes as a stopper. £100-150. $145-215

An exquisitely carved ribbed vase shaped bottle with a collared and decorated neck and ornate original contrast agate stopper. This is a high quality piece probably from the nineteenth century. £300-400. $430-575

This high shouldered agate bottle may have been the subject of an attempt to changes its color. The mock handles on the side and the small amount of pitting towards the foot show residues of what appears to be a colorant. This is typical of many snuff bottles. The natural red agate stopper appears to be original so the colorant may simply have been added to compliment it. £100-120. $145-175

A small dark area in this otherwise pale agate bottle bares a strong resemblance to a duck and as such makes it a highly desirable bottle. £250-300. $360-430

A simple dark brown agate bottle has been enhanced by the carving back of an outer pale layer in cameo form to reveal a bird sitting in a tree in spring blossom. *Courtesy of Penny Collection.* £75-100. $110-145

A pale gray agate miniature bottle upon which the outer layer of white has been carved back to reveal a fish, 1.25" (3 cm). *Courtesy of Penny Collection.* £80-100. $115-145

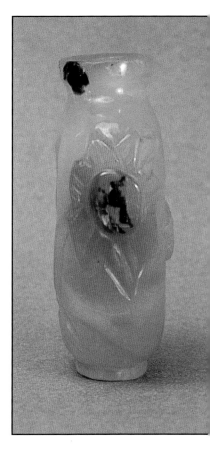

A beautifully translucent amber colored agate bottle with contrasting darker area lightly carved as a flower head. £80-100. $115-145

A beautifully carved pale brown and moss agate bottle of elegant proportions. £150-200. $215-285

A realistically shaped agate bottle in the form of a fish resting on its fins. Tiny eyes also of agate have been inset into the main body. £60-80. $85-115

Making full use of the contrasting colors in this agate pebble the carver has created an image of a child trying to catch a three-legged toad while holding onto a string of cash. Beneath the path on which the child is standing is a stream or pond in which fish are swimming. £150-200. $215-285

Shou Lao stands smiling holding a staff and a peach as usual. The bat which is resting beside his foot is in fact the stopper of this cleverly carved agate bottle in which a dark band has been used to form the staff. £150-200. $215-285

A simple banded agate bottle of large proportions. £50-60. $70-85

A cat seems an ideal subject for the mixed colors of this gray, yellow, and orange agate bottle. A hole in the center of its back suggests that the stopper was probably in the form of a mouse. £150-180. $215-260

A small agate snuff bottle. Middle Qing dynasty, eighteenth
century, 42 mm. (A) £8,000-12,000. $11,440-17,160

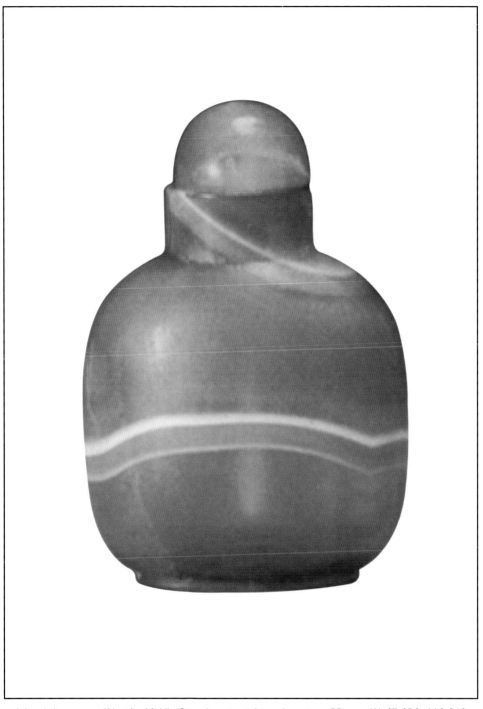

A banded agate snuff bottle. Middle Qing dynasty, eighteenth century, 55 mm. (A) £7,650. $10,940

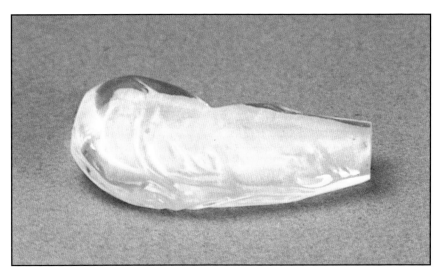

The asymmetrical gourd-like shape of this clear rock crystal bottle is carved with a shallow decoration of leaves and branches along one side. Its original stopper was probably in the form of the stem and calyx. £50-60. $70-85

A carved and pierced four-sided reticulated amethyst bottle of excellent color. The absence of an original stopper does not detract from this complex piece. £150-200. $215-285

A fine quartz crystal bottle in the form of the mythical three-legged toad, Chan, in whose mouth is clasped a large coin or cash which forms the stopper. £300-400. $430-575

The brown shading in this small nephrite bottle
enhances its appeal but to some it would be seen as a
fault. £40-50. $55-70

Mottled green and brown
nephrite make this squat
winter melon shaped bottle
attractive. *Courtesy of
Penny Collection.* £50-60.
$70-85

An almost white nephrite bottle of very elegant flattened vase shape with a tall neck. £150-180. $215-260

An elegant high shouldered pale green nephrite bottle with mock ring handles. £150-200. $215-285

An olive green nephrite bottle carved in the form of an elderly sage carrying a peach. His hat which also resembles a lotus leaf forms the stopper and his beneficient smile is a significant part of the bottle's symbolism. Courtesy of Penny Collection. £200-250. $285-360

A crudely carved but effective fish in pale green nephrite. Courtesy of Penny Collection. £50-70. $70-100

A mottled dark green chalcedony bottle in the form of a gourd with an integral ring around the waist. Such complex carving is not common and many pieces which would have had an integral ring have lost them to damage. £120-150. $175-215

A beautifully simple apple-green jadeite bottle, possibly color-enhanced, but nevertheless very desirable. *Courtesy of Penny Collection.* £150-200. $215-285

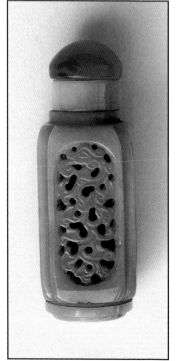

A square form pale green nephrite bottle with a reticulated pierced outer casing. The tight fitting nature of the outer section makes it appear impossible that it could have been carved to move. £120-150. $175-215

This very tactile dark green and brown nephrite bottle would have been some one's pride and joy. The colors on the flattened ovoid surfaces need no embellishments though a stylized dragon climbs each shoulder in relief. *Courtesy of Penny Collection.* £150-200. $215-285

An unusual amber-colored nephrite bottle with original stopper, simple in decoration, with mock ring handles to each shoulder. *Courtesy of Klemer Collection.* £100-120. $145-175

The bitter melon shape of this unusual nephrite bottle makes it an interesting collector's piece. The stopper incorporates both the stalk and the calyx. £120-150. $175-215

A slightly absurd looking subject as the two fish in this bottle are swimming side by side balancing the gourd on their heads. Even those experts in symbolism questioned on this subject were bemused by it. £100-120. $145-175

A finely carved white jade snuff bottle. Middle Qing dynasty, eighteenth century, 51 mm. (A) £3,500-4,500. $5,005-6,435

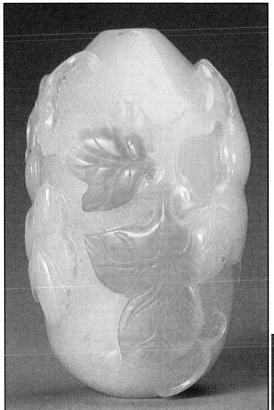

A celadon jade gourd-shaped snuff bottle. Middle Qing dynasty, eighteenth century, 63 mm. (A) £2,400-3,200. $3,435-4,580

A fine celadon jade melon-shaped snuff bottle. Middle Qing dynasty, eighteenth century, 50 mm. (A) £1,600-2,000. $2,290-2,860

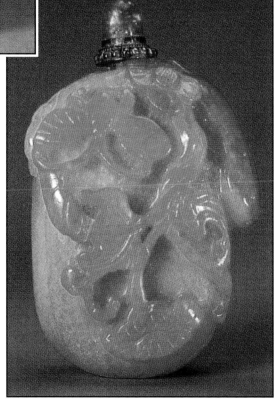

Two stylized dragons climb in high relief on this pale green jadeite bottle with original stopper. *Courtesy of Klemer Collection.* £100-120. $145-175

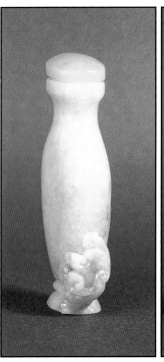

With an unusual flattene vase shape and equally unusual stopper and nec shape, it is difficult to decide whether this bott was made for use as a snuff bottle or for some other purpose. While it does not conform to usual snuff bottle parameters the exquisite work and color makes it prize part of this particular collection. The white jadeite with faint splashes of green has been carved to best advantage with a small lion dog in relief above the foot. Additional sligh engraving incorporates one of the green splashe into a vine leaf. *Courtesy of Klemer Collection.* £250-300. $360-430

Chapter Four
Glass Snuff Bottles

While the history of glass in China precedes that of snuff bottles by many centuries it was not until after their development that it became a home grown industry of any consequence. Prior to the *Qianlong* period, glass saw little use throughout China with most items that have been recorded or discovered having arrived with Arab traders or later from Europe. Even windows, which we take for granted in the West, were covered with paper rather than glass.

Apart from vessels and objects imported ready-made, little use was made of glass other than for decoration and then it was treated in the same way as precious or semi-precious stones. In fact it was the lapidary who generally worked glass well into the eighteenth and even the nineteenth-centuries.

Blocks of imported colored glass were cut, ground and polished in the same way as stone instead of being melted and re-worked under heat, as they would have been at their source. Items worked in this way were expensive and the craftsmanship greatly admired.

As a result early glass snuff bottles are rare and generally have simple designs and polishing with little or no carving or mixture of color. However, during the reign of the Emperor *Kangxi*, in the late seventeenth century, a German Jesuit priest, *Killian Stumpff*, and his colleagues transformed glass working in China and gave birth to what we now call *Peking Glass*.

These German experts developed or expanded the use of glass to form vessels of varying sizes but particularly snuff bottles, a firm favorite at Court. While lapidaries continued to work their own magic to produce the actual bottles, *Stumpff* and his fellows were allowed to set up a workshop in the Forbidden City where they decorated them and created wonderful objects to delight the Emperor.

Favorite of all seems to have been the cameo or overlay glass, which remains popular today, using one or more colors over the base bottle color to create contrasting patterns and pictures. The basic bottle, which, in later periods, may have been blown or molded and which may be clear, colored, frosted or bubbled, was then dipped in a glass of different color so that the outer layer eclipsed the inner. One or more further layers of color were then sometimes added before the cutting process began.

Most bottles recorded prior to the middle of the eighteenth century are simple ones of just one overlay color but later ones record up to four outer skins. As the layers of glass were carved and polished away the cameo pattern emerged with sometimes spectacular results. Although generally termed carving the process is one of polishing and cutting against a grinding bit of various grades of coarseness and size. Now operated with the help of electricity they were formerly controlled using a treadle machine. Some of the finer craftsmen, who are more concerned with quality than speed, still use this method as it gives them more control and lessens the risk of the glass fragmenting.

Although generically known as *Peking Cameo Glass* much of this type is recorded as having come from *Boshan* in *Shandong* Province. In fact it is only these latter bottles which give us an insight into the actual makers because in the Peking workshops it was unheard of to have any dedication other than that of the Emperor. By contrast some of the *Shandong* makers signed with their own names, especially in later years.

With all cameo glass bottles, early or late, it is the quality of craftsmanship that needs to be examined. Many bottles are crudely and clumsily decorated. In early examples this may be forgiven as the art was still being perfected but in later ones it is simply a sign of cheapness. Fine detail and skilled design shine out when the better bottles are held against their cruder companions. Of particular note are pieces which have further decoration added to the innermost layer of the bottle. This is often in the form of stylized waves or intricate patterns and is very difficult to achieve, as it must be cut in between the cameo decoration already completed.

Much debate exists among serious collectors as to when blown and molded bottles took over from the cut and polished ones produced by the lapidary. As late as 1770, long after their arrival, however, the Jesuits recorded that even though a great many bottles were being produced, "nothing was blown."

The development of glass working particularly in relation to snuff bottles went far beyond the dipping and carving of the cameo style. It seems to have been a constant challenge spurred on by successive Emperors' enthusiasm and demands to produce ever more complex and imaginative pieces.

Using combinations of colors, ground stone pigment, stretching, blowing, chemical additives and imagination the art was expanded so that glass emulated stone and was so convincing that even today some bottles are incorrectly described. Agate and jade were popular stones to imitate, as they were so highly prized, though the aim does not seem to have been deceit but rather the expansion and expression of the glass worker's skill.

With glass working being a constantly expanding and developing process it is frequently difficult to date precisely the examples that are encountered. It is often said that a bottle is so complex it must be a late one. This may or may not be true.

A type that frequently attracts awe from new collectors and admirers is the multi-colored but not multi-layered bottle. Here the cameo effect is present in several colors on one base with spectacular effect. In fact the technique is simpler than a dipped bottle with either blobs or strips of glass of various colors being applied to the outside before being carved individually. They are nonetheless attractive and highly prized.

Equally highly prized, though not always deservedly, are bottles referred to as Imperial Yellow. This opaque yellow color, also referred to by the Chinese as chicken fat or chicken oil yellow, was a favorite of the Emperor *Qianlong* who decreed that it was only to be used by his court. Silk covers for the royal thrones and many of his and later Emperors' robes show a continued interest in the color. In later reigns, however, the decree forbidding use by commoners was either retracted or disregarded so some bottles of this color emerged and joined less esteemed collections.

The list of possible examples in glass, as in other materials, is so wide and diverse that it is impractical to show them all but those illustrated should give the reader an idea of what to look for and perhaps set some goals for a collection.

Simple amber glass bottle with stylized dragon shoulders. *Courtesy of Skippen Collection.* £60-80. $85-115

Carved amber glass in the form of a long-eared Chinese Buddha. *Courtesy of Skippen Collection.* £60-80. $85-115

An unusually subtle amber glass bottle carved in the shape of a peach. £40-50. $55-70

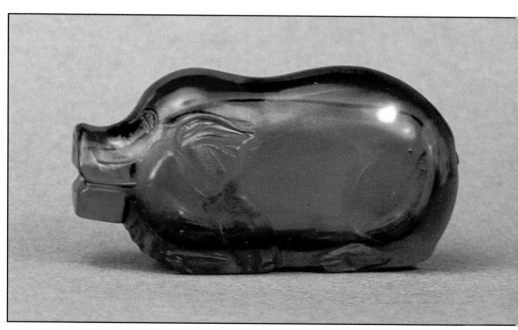

Amber glass bottle carved in the form of a friendly pig. £80-100. $115-145

Plain milk glass bottle in a silvered metal casing with filigreed butterfly detail. £60-80. $85-115

Carved blue glass image of the Immortal Shou Lao. £80-100. $115-145

A clear glass crystal fish with excellent detail resting horizontally on fins. *Courtesy of Penny Collection.* £150-200. $215-285

Subtly carved in pale amber glass, this monkey is clinging to a peach. *Courtesy of Penny Collection.* £80-100. $115-145

A rather comical bottle carved in the form of a green glass tortoise carrying a golden glass boat shaped cash. It might be assumed that the cash forms the stopper but it is attached to the back of the tortoise, the mouth of the bottle being the mouth of the animal. *Courtesy of Penny Collection.* £80-100. $115-145

Carved amber glass Buddha head in an Indian style. *Courtesy of Penny Collection.* £80-100. $115-145

Carved amber glass fish standing upright on a curled tail resting upon a stylized cushion of water. £100-120. $145-175

Hexagonal carved amber glass bottle with faceted shoulders. £80-100. $115-145

Turquoise blue glass bottle in cylindrical form with a narrowed neck. Wear indicates age and the simple style is very tactile. £120-150. $175-215

Imperial yellow ribbed melon shaped bottle with double neck. £80-100. $115-145

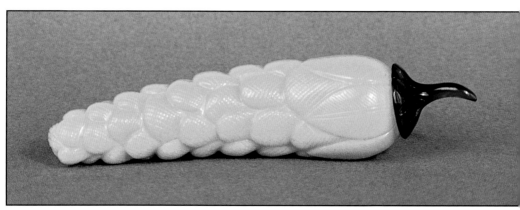

A naturalistic vegetable is carved in Imperial yellow with a green glass stem stopper. *Courtesy of Penny Collection.* £100-120. $145-175

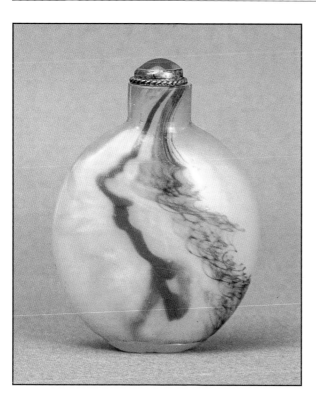

Milk glass bottle with yellow, red, and brown twisted detail. Style and wear indicate age probably late nineteenth century. £100-150. $145-215

Amber glass with gold flecks make this double-waisted bottle unusual. Wear indicates age. £120-150. $175-215

Milk glass bottle twisted with red and blue *mille fiori* canes. £120-150. $175-215

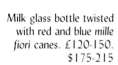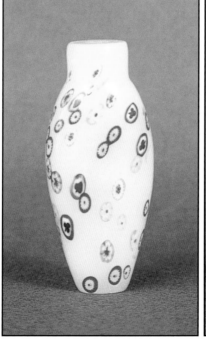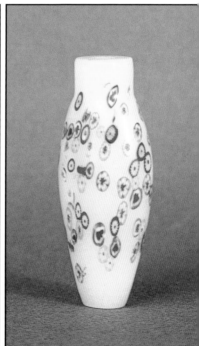

A very tactile black glass bottle twisted with infused goldstone.
Probably nineteenth century. £150-200. $215-285

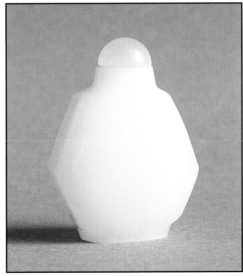

Simple but unusual faceted milk glass bottle
simulating fine white jade. Slight wear indicates
some age. £100-120. $145-175

A lovely mottled green glass bottle simulating jade and
showing signs of age. £100-150. $145-215

Three simple milk glass bottles overlaid with contrasting color and carved back to reveal insects. Subtle carving makes these three excellent examples of the quality of some of the modern work. *Courtesy of Skippen Collection.* £60-80 each. $85-115

Two clear and blue glass bottles show detail on the clear inner bottle. The dragonflies are hovering above rippling water and the spider is suspended on a clear glass web. *Courtesy of Skippen Collection.* £60-80. $85-115

Three good cameo bottles, the red showing a selection of insects on a bulbous bottle. The green, several stylized dragons at play and the amethyst, a stylized dragon on each side. *Courtesy of Skippen Collection.* £50-60 each. $70-85 each

Two bottles showing finely carved color over white milk glass, the red with a traditional four-toed dragon and the blue with carp swimming among pond weed. *Courtesy of Skippen Collection.* £50-60 each. $70-85 each

Small red and clear bottle with inverted lotus petal decoration, 1.25" (4 cm). *Courtesy of Skippen Collection.* £40-50. $55-70

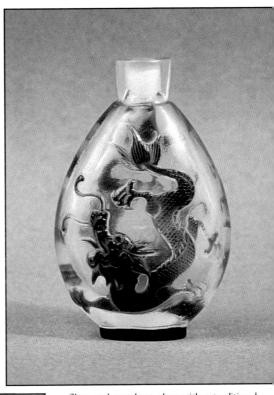

Clear and amethyst glass with a traditional dragon on each side. Good scale detail. *Courtesy of Skippen Collection.* £40-60. $55-85

Milk and green glass decoration depicting a proud chicken standing on a basket overseeing chicks. *Courtesy of Skippen Collection.* £40-60. $55-85

Green and clear glass with a Tang prancing horse on each side and bamboo style decoration from the shoulders to the foot. *Courtesy of Skippen Collection.* £60-80. $85-115

Gourd shaped clear and blue glass design depicting fish swimming in a pond of floating weed with stylized wave decoration on the inner bottle. *Courtesy of Penny Collection.* £50-60. $70-85

Milk white bottle with black overlay carved with fantailed carp in a pond with lotus flowers and leaves. *Courtesy of Penny Collection.* £40-50. $55-70

Pretty milk and red overlay with downward hanging leaf collar and blossom in each segment. *Courtesy of Penny Collection.* £40-50. $55-70

A clear glass bottle appears to sit comfortably in the green overlay cut to imitate a plant holder. *Courtesy of Penny Collection.* £40-50. $55-70

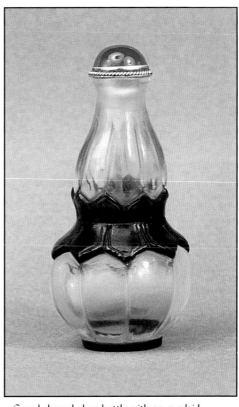

Gourd shaped clear bottle with an overlaid green waist band and foot. £40-50. $55-70

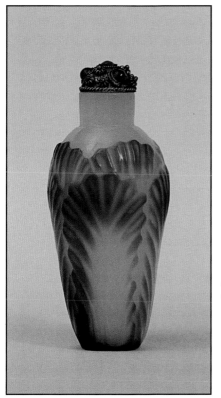

A milk glass inner overlaid with light green and delicately carved as a Chinese cabbage. £40-50. $55-70

A clear bottle with the green outer layer carved back to reveal a basket of fish. Excellent detail in the cord forming the basket handle. £50-60. $70-85

The reverse show two stylized drag preparing to fight The imagery of th bottle would sug it wishes the own strength and pati in an adversarial situation.

Milk glass bottle with overlaid amethyst color carved to reveal a crane standing on the back of a mythical tortoise. Additional carved detail to shoulders and sides. £80-100. $115-145

A tall narrow clear bottle overlaid with simple blue decoration, 4.5" (10.5 cm). £50-60. $70-85

This amusing clear and blue glass bottle in the form of a tortoise shows an interesting combination of symbolism and humor. The shell detail is carefully engraved onto the inner layer while a blue crane or stork lies on the tortoise's back. Beneath the bottle the tortoise has elongated legs and human-like feet. £80-100. $115-145

A large amethyst colored carp curls beneath a clear bulbous bottle. *Courtesy of Penny Collection.* £50-60. $70-85

An angry red snake curls around this opaque white vase shaped bottle. £40-50. $55-70

A large cabinet or table bottle in clear glass overlaid with amethyst. The continuous landscape shows cranes on rocks with clouds in the background. The neck is surrounded by a collar of palm leaves and the whole appears to rest on a four-footed stand, 4" (10 cm). £100-120. $145-175

A clear and blue glass bottle with horse and beaded decoration. £40-50. $55-70

Two typical inexpensive clear bottles overlaid with red. £30-40 each. $40-55

The heads of four bulls are carved in blue relief on this clear bottle. £30-40. $40-55

A blue dragon adorns this simple clear bottle. £30-40. $40-55

A simple blue and clear bottle which could be used in the same way as a birthday card. The large character depicted wishes long life but is carved with the appearance of a fish skeleton in the hope that the recipient will also eat well. Additional images of a bat and dragon to either side of the character enhance the good wishes. £40-50. $55-70

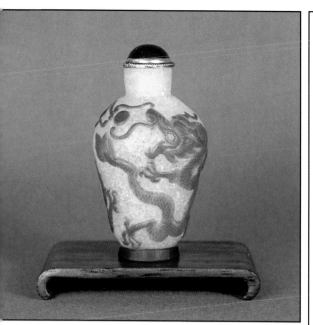

A simple two-layered bottle with fiery red outer layer aptly chosen to depict two dragons fighting over a pearl. £40-50. $55-70

A narrow flat milk glass bottle overlaid with a thin coating of amethyst carved with a continuous scene of birds flying over a rocky landscape among clouds. £40-50. $55-70

Three-layered bottle consisting of a milk glass inner with red and yellow outer layers. The scene is one of a sage with his students in a wooded landscape beside a lake. *Courtesy of Skippen Collection.* £100-120. $145-175

A milk glass bottle overlaid with red and then black. The black remains dominant and the red is used for highlights and small detail. Both sides show images of men in boats traveling or fishing. £100-120. $145-175

A superbly carved three-layered bottle of milk glass and then red and a further layer of white overlay beautifully carved with a stork or crane, lotus leaves and chrysanthemum flowers. £150-160. $215-230

A beautifully detailed three-layered white and green bottle carved with one of the Immortals standing on a cloud beneath the moon and other clouds. £150-160. $215-230

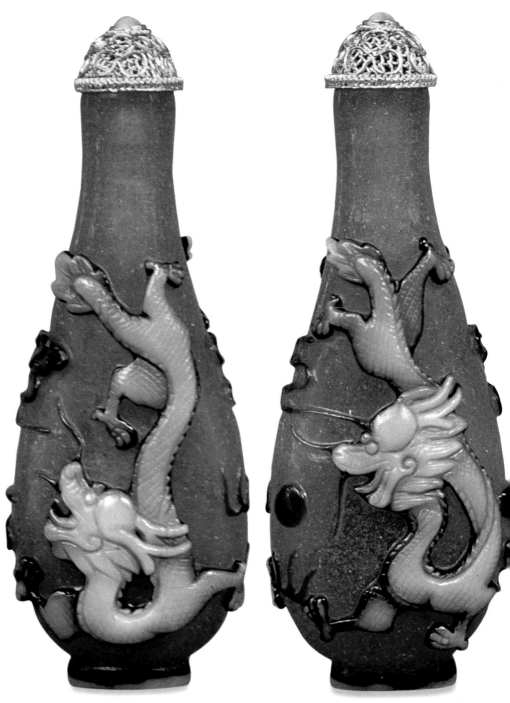

The use of cranberry, amethyst and opaque white give this dragon bottle a distinct quality and style. The carver has made maximum use of the overlay effects of the chosen colors. £150-160. $215-230

A three-layered pink, green, and white bottle lavishly carved with a flying butterfly. £100-120. $145-175

Opaque pink inner bottle overlaid with white and then green carved in beautiful detail to show a peacock in full display. £100-120. $145-175

A tall, flattened opaque white bottle overlaid with amethyst and a further layer of white. On one side it depicts a man fishing in a lake symbolizing plenty and tranquility. On the other side a man rides home through a field of sheep. A line of characters decorates one side reading *Yu Sun Yue zhi*, the "*zhi*" meaning "made by" and the remainder the carver's name. A fictional Qianlong reign mark also adorns the bottle indicating its style origins. £150-160. $215-230

A three-layered red and white bottle beautifully carved with landscape and figures depicting life in the southern mountains. £150-160. $215-230

A lovely three-layered green and white bottle depicting the lucky symbol of a monkey riding a horse. £140-150. $200-215

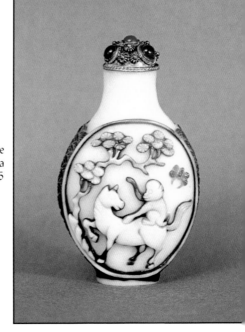

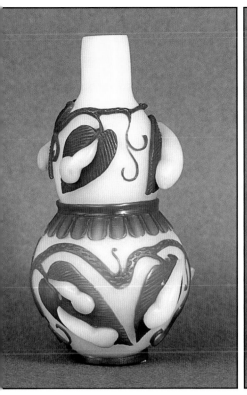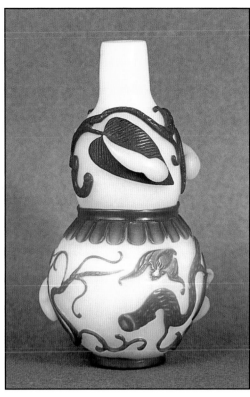

A large blue and white gourd shaped table bottle in two colors with thickly applied blobs of additional white glass as an outer layer. These are carved as gourds fruiting on the blue vines which entwine the bottle. A single large bat is seen in the lower section, 5" (12 cm). £100-120. $145-175

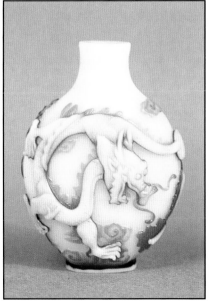

A dragon and phoenix are beautifully carved in deep relief on opposite sides of this three-layered bottle. The opaque white sandwiching the red is highly vibrant and effective. £150-160. $215-230

An unusually dark three-layered bottle with an opaque green inner overlaid with white and then black. The carving reveals fishermen beneath overhanging trees and a man on horseback leaving his mountain retreat. The simple oval seal is repeated on both sides and reads *"jie yang"*, a form of good luck. £150-160. $215-230

Opposite page, bottom: Milk glass with an overlay of green and splashes of black and red. Carved in the form of a Chinese fruit with an insect resting upon it. Matching stalk stopper is missing. *Courtesy of Penny Collection.* £60-80. $85-115

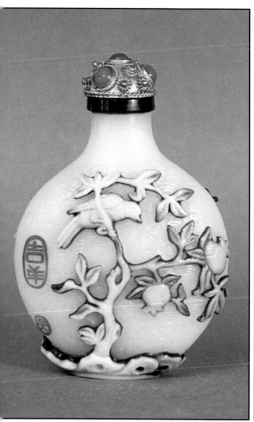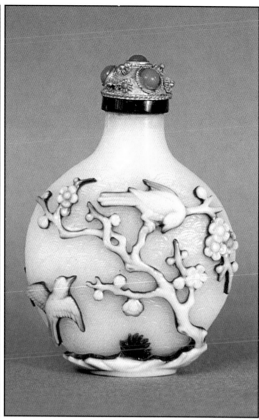

Two birds and the *mei hua* flower herald the end of winter and the beginning of spring and on the other side a single bird and *shi liu* (pomegranate) complete the imagery of good luck from beginning to end or throughout the year. The large oval seal *"jie yang"* wishes good luck and the small circular one reads *"xiong"* ("big brother") probably the carver's actual or adopted name. £150-160. $215-230

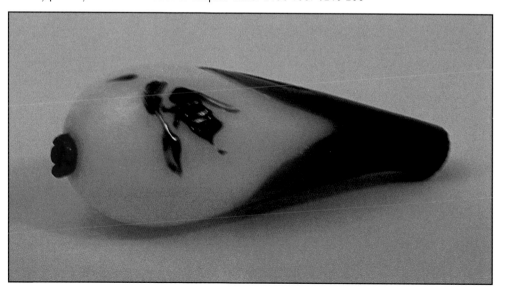

A rare five color overlay glass snuff bottle. Middle Qing dynasty, eighteenth century, 57 mm. (A) £7,000-8,500. $10,010-12,155

Chapter Five
Enameled Snuff Bottles

Foremost among snuff bottles throughout their history have been the enamels. This group includes painted and applied enamel decorations that are fired after the application of the color in order to "fix" it on to the material base of the bottle. For this reason the enamel grouping includes porcelain, metals of all kinds and glass. The latter proved problematic because the required temperature for firing the enamels was very close to the melting point of the glass and hence many experimental pieces ended their days as a sad heap at the bottom of the kiln.

To simplify the understanding of enamels they should be broken down into several categories with each having its own history and development.

1. Cloisonné

Sometimes referred to as enamel filigreeing but better known as *cloisonné*, this is generally recognized as an almost uniquely oriental art practiced mostly in China and Japan. Having been developed since the Yuan dynasty and probably imported as part of the Arabic trade, *cloisonné* involves the laying of fine wires (generally copper) onto a metal body (also usually copper) to create a filigreed effect. Some, if not all, of the gaps between the wires, set out in a pattern, are then filled with powdered semi-precious stones and subsequently fired at very high temperature to create the enamel which may be one or two millimeters thick.

The post-firing item, be it snuff bottle or vase looks little like the finished product as it requires fairly aggressive polishing to remove the excess enamels and make them level with the wires or *cloisons*. Once polished the end product is colorful and exquisite.

The small nature of snuff bottles means that they were not ideally suited to this type of decoration so the number available either old or modern are few. A small and expensive number were made with silver wire on either bronze or silver bodies.

2. Metals

More suited to the purpose is enamel painting on metal, the technique for which was imported from Europe during the reign of the Emperor *Kangxi*. The majority of these bottles are also on copper bodies though gold, silver and bronze examples are known.

The decoration of enamel paints is applied by brush to a white or generally light colored ground of enamel slip which is then fused into a single enamel coating by firing at high temperature. This technique is often referred to in Europe as *champlevé* enamel and known in its Chinese form as Canton enamel.

While the latter name is aptly given because a high percentage of the enameling was done in Canton (Guangzhou) the majority of the pieces in the Imperial collection were crafted in the Forbidden City's own workshops set up on the Emperor's instructions.

To satisfy the desire for European style enamels the French enameller *Gravereau* was invited to Peking (Beijing) in 1717 by the Emperor *Kangxi* already in the fifty-eighth year of his reign. Sadly many of the records from this era were destroyed but there are only ten bottles, which bear the appropriate reign mark, known to exist from this period.

Imperial enthusiasm grew for this type of bottle and additional workshops were set up to meet demand. Output, however, was still not on a scale that one might expect today and each bottle took a great deal of time to perfect. During the *Qianlong* period many bottles were made with western or pseudo-western designs including fashionable people and European style houses and landscapes.

Regular production of painted enamel bottles in and for the Imperial Court came almost to an end around 1796 after orders from the Emperor *Jiaqing* to that effect. They continued to be produced in Guangzhou and in the late Qing dynasty enamel workshops reappeared in the capital imitating bottles of previous reigns. While the artistry is not considered to be as high as the earlier ones from the Imperial workshops, it would take an expert or accurate provenance to discern them especially as many were marked with the earlier reign marks as a tribute to the originals.

3. Glass

The third category of enamels are those on glass bodies. As already mentioned the firing temperature for the enamels is close to the melting point of the glass. It was therefore necessary to do a great deal of experimentation, using various ingredients, to raise the temperature at which the glass would be destroyed but sufficient for the enamel to fuse. There was some success and as a result a lovely range of enameled glass bottles emerged.

Most are decorated with elaborate tracery patterns which enabled the colors to remain separate instead of blending, as they tend to, under the heat. Others have been carved before the enameling so that the added color highlights the detail of the carving.

Most of these bottles were the result of collaboration between the different workshops set up for glass work and enameling, as the skills are so very different.

4. Porcelain

In a bid to be accurate it should be said that some porcelain bottles are enameled rather than painted and then glazed. The distinction is made because the firing of the enamel decoration forms the glaze itself without the need for a separate glaze to be applied as it is when using paints.

Enamels are most often used for additional surface decoration after the first firing to harden the glaze and protect the under-glaze painting. When enamel is applied in small dots or gem shaped designs this is often referred to as beading or jewelling. Few examples exist, perhaps because the technique is very protracted and risks damaging a bottle that might otherwise be regarded as finished.

Famille rose enamels painted on an opaque white glass bottle depict a large pink lotus flower with its petals deliberately resembling the shape of a peach. A blue ribbon and a butterfly both flutter behind the flower. On the reverse the decoration is a large green lotus leaf with a white butterfly. Courtesy of Penny Collection. £80-100. $115-145

Elaborate and finely applied blue tracery surrounds two stylized dragons in a background of "rice" dots. The use of a strong Imperial yellow enamel highlights the decoration on this bottle beautifully. £100-120. $145-175

A white milk glass bottle with monochrome painted enamel showing a lady on a chair looking at an opium pipe on one side and on the reverse, she is seen relaxing on an opium bed with her husband. Both are smoking opium pipes. £60-80. $85-115

Three ladies with bound feet appear in this monochrome enamel painting on an opaque white bottle. £60-80. $85-115

An opaque white glass bottle with a monochrome image painted in enamels of a lady tempted by the opium pipe in front of her. £60-80. $85-115

A fairly modern brown glass bottle with enamel decoration designed to contain medicines. This shows that the tradition of medicine dispensed in this form continues today and still warrants elaborately decorated bottles. An interesting addition to a collection. £20-30. $30-40

A clear glass bottle prettily decorated on both sides with images of enameled deer. £50-60. $70-85

A carved clear glass bottle enameled mostly in yellow depicts a basket containing two freshly caught fish. *Courtesy of Penny Collection.* £100-120. $145-175

A carved cylindrical opaque white glass bottle with the relief areas highlighted with painted enamels. The subject is spring blossom and bamboo. £50-60. $70-85

A cylindrical *cloisonné* enamel bottle with unusually dark background and floral decoration on a copper body. *Courtesy of Penny Collection.* £50-60. $70-85

A painted enamel on copper bottle in "Canton" style with an unusually dark background depicting a dragon. £25-35. $35-50

A cylindrical copper bottle with painted enamel decorations in European style. The naked woman would not be a traditional Chinese decoration and this is a bottle created for the modern market with an interest in erotica. £15-25. $25-35

Two gourd shaped copper bottles hand-painted in enamels in the "Canton" style. These are interesting though inexpensive examples of a revived art. £25-30. $35-40

Chapter Six
Porcelain Snuff Bottles

Although already mentioned briefly, under the heading of enamels, porcelain forms a major part of the snuff bottle range. Established for hundreds of years before the snuff bottle even came into being the porcelain factories of China were not slow to recognise a new market. Their major export trade to Europe was well established by this stage as well as a highly lucrative home market for both fine porcelain and domestic wares.

A full history of porcelain and other Chinese ceramics is a major undertaking in itself and the curious collector will have no shortage of reference both inside and outside the snuff bottle publications. It is sufficient for our purposes here to categorise porcelain as follows:-

Underglaze decoration

This involves the application of color, by brush or other means, in a suspended powder form, rather like water colors, and the subsequent firing of the article with a clear overglaze. In the process the colors are fused between the glaze and the porcelain and in doing so some, such as cobalt, change their hue. Cobalt changes from the applied black to the familiar blue associated with Chinese ceramics. Failure to fire properly may leave some areas of decoration black, if the temperature hasn't been high enough, or smudged blue if the temperature has been too high.

This type of decoration is seen in all types of ceramics and forms the largest element of the export wares so popular in Europe and around the world today. Although some colors such as cobalt blue and iron red may appear together this is difficult to achieve because of the differing fireing temperatures required for good results. Red and blue underglaze is therefore fairly uncommon and explains why in most porcelain decoration the blue is underglaze and the red applied as an overglaze enamel.

Enameled decoration

Often referred to as Canton enamel or Famille Rose these colors are applied after the first glaze fireing or sometimes instead of it. This type of "overglaze" painting can be seen independently of, or sometimes with, underglaze painting.

Colored and special effect glazes

These have also been a feature of Chinese ceramics for centuries, even before the discovery of porcelain, so it was reasonable to expect that they would appear as part of the choice of snuff bottles.

Colored glazes often enhance relief decoration or carving on the porcelain and form different layers of shade as the applied thickness varies. Such glazes may also be enhanced by deliberate crackling effects which give the impression of ancient origins and deterioration. These are not an attempt at deceipt but an integral part of the range of glazes used by the Chinese for centuries.

Colored clays

Most Chinese porcelain is white but occasionally colors are introduced or the natural color of the clay is enhanced. Most often encountered is *Yi Xing* which looks like red or black terracotta but is technically a type of porcelain. The majority of items falling into the *Yi Xing* category are tea pots but there are a very small number of snuff bottles which have applied enamels.

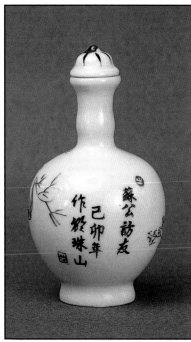

This selection of porcelain bottles have been hand-painted with enamels over the glaze and then re-fired. The quality of the workmanship is surprisingly good for the market at which they have been aimed. The subjects are stories from Chinese history and mythology and reflect ideas of morals and personal status. Prices do vary but should be buyable between £30 and £50. Lower quality imitations may have applied transfers or very poor quality painting and can be purchased for as little as £5. However, once compared with the better quality versions they will have little interest for most collectors.

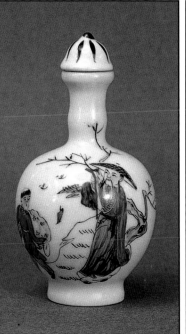

An inexpensive four-sided porcelain bottle decorated with Cantonese style enamels. £30-40. $40-55

Four similar Cantonese enamel bottles with domestic scenes moderately well painted and ideally priced for starting a modest collection. *Courtesy of Li, Jin, and Yan Collection. Photo by Ma Jun.* £30-40 each. $40-55

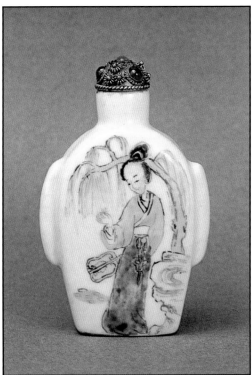

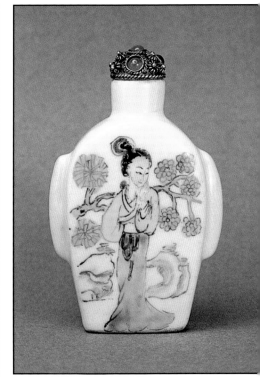

Two elegant ladies standing beneath trees are the subjects of this delicately enameled bottle. £25-35. $35-50

A very simple nineteenth century plain white porcelain bottle with delicate monochrome image of a horse in over-glaze enamel. Extensive use has rubbed the surface of the outer enamel but the bottle remains attractive. £80-100. $115-145

An unusual, and impracti-cal, teapot shaped bottle molded with considerable relief detail. The bulk of the body has been silvered while the flat panels are enameled. £100-120. $145-175

A molded bottle in the form of an elephant decorated in bright enameled colors. The outline of the relief detail has been highlighted with fine brown tracery. £25-35. $35-50

A white crackle-glazed porcelain bottle. £40-60. $55-85

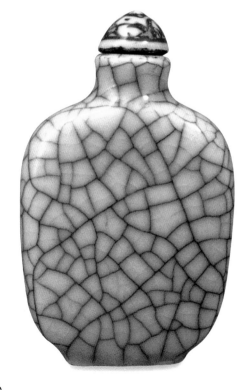

This exquisitely decorated porcelain bottle shows the continued standard of workmanship which is available in some twentieth century pieces. The delicacy of the brush strokes on the flattened panels and the rich colors of the sides show considerable skill. The two pictorial panels show kittens at play, one in the garden having caught a butterfly and the others beside a lotus pond looking at the fish. The additional flower decoration and gilding which appear on this bottle are of excellent quality. £200-250. $285-360

A *famille rose* porcelain snuff bottle. Qing dynasty, nineteenth
century, 55 mm. (A) £1,100-1,300. $1,575-1,860

A *famille rose* porcelain snuff bottle. Mark and period of Qianlong
(1736-1795), 59 mm. (A) £1,500-1,750. $2,145-2,505

Made in the form of the "*pí pa*", a Chinese instrument, this unusual bottle is delicately enameled. A four character "*Guangxu*" reign mark acknowledges the artist's inspiration and the implied age of the original bottle. £200-250. $285-360

A lavish white porcelain bottle with enamel decoration of flowers, butterflies and a bird. The base carries Qianlong style reign mark. *Courtesy of Penny Collection.* £200-250. $285-360

An iron-red porcelain snuff bottle.
Qing dynasty Daoguang (1821-
1850), 57 mm. (A) £813. $1,165

These are three pretty but modern white porcelain bottles, two with under-glaze red and the other with Cantonese enamel decoration. All are hand-painted and of good quality. *Courtesy of Li, Jin, and Yan Collection. Photo by Ma Jun.* £40-50 each. $55-70

Any book on Chinese porcelain will highlight the difficultly of firing cobalt and iron oxide (to produce blue and red) under the glaze. Even some inexpensive bottles however, are available with this combination though they are not particularly easy to find. £40-50. $55-70

A molded porcelain double fish bottle with under-glaze blue and red decoration. £50-60. $70-85

Simple blue and white bottle with splashes of under-glaze iron-red to highlight the flowers. £25-35. $35-50

Shaped like many nineteenth century porcelain tea caddies but with an elongated neck, this bottle has been delicately painted in under-glaze blue. £30-40. $40-55

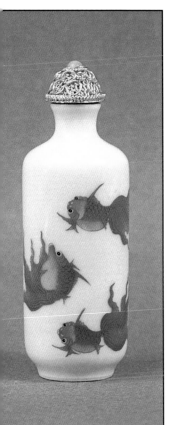

Typical fantail fish decoration in under-glaze red is here highlighted with areas of gold. A simple but well executed bottle. £40-50. $55-70

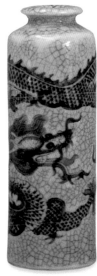

Carefully controlled crackling which has acquired brown highlight enhances the cobalt blue against the remaining white areas of this bottle. The tall cylindrical shape is simple but effective. £50-60. $70-85

Two crudely decorated bone white bottles, possibly intended for medicine rather than snuff, but certainly, made for the lower class market. £30-40 each. $40-55

A large flattened double gourd shaped bottle with celadon glaze over "wu cai" (five color) decoration. The areas highlighted with color are also lightly in relief, 5.0" (13 cm). £60-80. $85-115

A reticulated bottle with cylindrical inner container visible through a heart shaped window. The painting shows two men playing chess in an open landscape. A Qianlong reign mark appears on the base. *Courtesy of Klemer Collection.* £120-150. $175-215

Three late Qing porcelain bottles hand-painted in cobalt blue under-glaze, two with additional underglaze iron-red decoration. The smallest bottle shows two small repairs which are fairly typical of some bottles of this period. *Courtesy of Li, Jin, and Yan Collection. Photo by Ma Jun.* £250-300 each (damaged bottle, £100-120). $145-175

An unusual white porcelain bottle from the late Qing dynasty with under-glaze blue and red decoration. This bottle carries a Chinese government wax export seal which means that the item may legally be removed from China. Such seals appear on many articles and are not, as sometimes claimed, a guarantee of age but simply of legal exportability. *Courtesy of Li, Jin, and Yan Collection. Photo by Ma Jun.* £300-350. $430-500

Two molded porcelain figure bottles of the Buddha and *Shou Lao* are typical of a series of similar characters. For the price their workmanship and appeal make them well worth buying. £30-50. $40-70

Over-glaze enamels decorate this charming little bottle which depicts a fierce female lion dog with her baby sitting on a boat shaped cash which is decorated with flowers. £30-40. $40-55

A baby turtle emerging from its egg is the inspiration for this lovely piece. The accuracy in both the molding and the painting is very appealing. £100-150. $145-215

A crudely decorated molded bottle depicting a male and female couple standing beside a tree. £20-30. $30-40

A molded and carved figure bottle of an elderly mystic decorated in "wu cai" (five color) enamels. £50-60. $70-85

A molded porcelain elephant hand-painted to enhance the relief decoration. £40-60. $55-85

A black and white oil spot style decoration enhances this naturalistic double gourd shaped bottle. £40-50. $55-70

A *famille rose* porcelain snuff bottle. Middle Qing dynasty, eighteenth century, 57 mm. (A) £1,913. $2,735

The dark green glaze on this small relief molded bottle has been rubbed with extensive use indicating that this is probably a nineteenth century piece and that it was well used. £60-80. $85-115

A European porcelain bottle with applied fragmented porcelain under the glaze made in the form of a snuff bottle but perhaps intended for perfume. Such bottles do sometimes appear in China and may have been exported in an attempt to infiltrate the snuff bottle market. £20-30. $30-40

Molded in the form of a child clutching a large fish around which is a base decorated with lotus leaves and flowers. This bottle has a heavy turquoise-colored glaze. £40-50. $55-70

A European porcelain bottle (probably German), delicately decorated with an applied transfer, typical of a group of items exported to China in the late nineteenth century with the apparent intention of gaining a foothold in the snuff bottle market. By the time this occurred, however, the market was already waning. £20-30. $30-40

A pale celadon glaze carved porcelain bottle with deep relief detail and a cash shaped neck. This new bottle has been dirtied to give it age but is nevertheless of good quality workmanship. *Courtesy of Li, Jin, and Yan Collection. Photo by Ma Jun.* £30-40. $40-55

A simple cream glazed porcelain bottle with lion head and mock ring handles in the style of a Song dynasty jar. Probably nineteenth century. *Courtesy of Penny Collection.* £80-100. $115-145

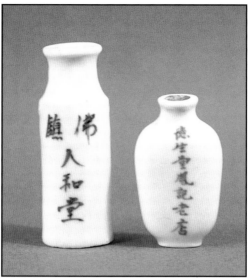

A simple cylindrical medicine bottle with five characters reading "fo zhen ren he tang translating as "Buddhist temple people happy room". This is clearly a reference to a temple dispensary. On the reverse of the bottle are the characters "ba bao dan" ("eight goodness tablets") where the use of the word "dan" indicates their very tiny size. Many temples produced and dispensed medicines in this way as part of their income and would have had bottles especially made in local workshops in the same way as modern drug companies. £30-40. $40-55

A heavily worn larger box-like bottle which has not originated from a temple. The name emphasizes the Han origins of the doctor, which to some people, may have been important. The characters read "Zhen Han", "Wu liang jin" (the doctor's name from the "Wu" family) and "zhi de tang", translating as "very good helpful place", which would have been the name of the surgery. £40-50. $55-70

Chapter Seven
A Hotchpotch of Other Materials

To give a definitive list of other materials used for snuff bottles would be almost impossible because someone would always have a variation to add.

The following pages show as many examples as have been available to us but offer a very comprehensive range which includes natural bottles made from fruit stones, bamboo, wood and coral as well as those in bronze, silver, bone, horn, lacquer, and of course ivory. Particularly elegant and popular are a few made from natural lacquer built up in hundreds of layers on a copper body.

In this category as much detail as possible is given with each example so that the reader can see and understand without having to flick from page to page. It is not surprising that such bottles were very popular among the Qing Court and remain so with modern collectors because these are among the most tactile of all and even quite early examples need not be expensive because they are not considered by many to be important enough to fight over at auction.

A double gourd shaped carved horn bottle with an inset ivory panel. The panel itself is engraved with the image of a young lady which is reinforced by the characters "shi nu" ("beautiful girl"). On the reverse, high-lighted in gold, are the characters "shi nu yang sheng" ("the beautiful girl is resting to regain her energy"). *Courtesy of Klemer Collection.* £120-150. $175-215

A color enhanced branch coral bottle carved with the head of a lion looking around a tree trunk. £100-120. $145-175

An unknown creature peers from the base of this branch coral bottle. £100-120. $145-175

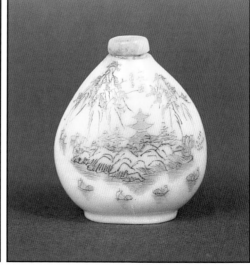

A simple tagua nut bottle with engraved and colored detail of a phoenix and landscape. *Courtesy of Klemer Collection.* £25-30. $35-40

The modern use of the tagua nut as a replacement for ivory makes a refreshing change from resins and plastics. Like ivory it must be carved and having been baked it is quite hard and brittle. Many of the carvings are quite simplistic and cheap but some like this ribbed melon snuff bottle show the continued quality of the carver's art. Engraved and painted. *Courtesy of Klemer Collection.* £40-50. $55-70

Carved dense unprocessed cork is an unusual choice of material for this bottle which has been shaped like a rock and decorated with small plants, including one which forms the stopper. It also carries an erotic image of a naked man and woman taking advantage of the rock to hide their activities. £80-100. $115-145

The elegant carving on this dark wooden bottle might be considered to be *art nouveau* if it were western in origin. It is possible that the carver encountered such influences before creating this lovely image of lotus with ducks and cranes. *Courtesy of Penny Collection.* £80-100. $115-145

A finely carved boxwood bottle depicting a boy riding an ox. £50-60. $70-85

A tall turned wood bottle, probably for storage and decanting to a smaller container, which dates from the late nineteenth century. The simplicity is an attractive feature, 4.0" (10 cm). £80-100. $115-145

The carved basket weave of this old wooden bottle has acquired the pattination which only age can give it. The question, however, which is more important is whether it was made simply for use as a wooden bottle or as a template for something more valuable. A great deal of skill has been applied to the carving suggesting that it was, in fact, a template possibly made for the approval of the Emperor himself. £120-150. $175-215

Opposite page, bottom right: A boxwood figure carving of a dog. The head removes as the stopper and the entire body is hollowed. The lack of ability to bend a spoon around the corner into the dog's body suggests that this bottle was never intended for actual use. £50-60. $70-85

A charming boxwood bottle carved in deep relief on both sides. £50-60. $70-85

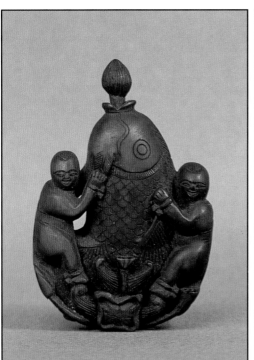

A dark stained carved boxwood figure bottle of two boys holding an enormous fish. *Courtesy of Penny Collection.* £50-60. $70-85

A small bamboo bottle which was probably used to sell a commercial brand of snuff to be used either directly or decanted into a more ornate version. In archaic form the characters read "*qí sang*" translating as "strange/different enjoy". This brand name or variety name is enhanced on the opposite side by an engraving of winter plum blossom which in itself symbolizes life through winter or adversity. Nineteenth century. £40-50. $55-70

A small bronze bottle with a relief panel depicting an ox. A tall foot and turquoise and coral beads inset into the shoulders give it a distinctive character. And a similar bronze bottle with a pair of fish, but without the stone embellishments. £80-100 each. $115-145

An octagonal tortoise shell bottle probably on a delicate wooden body, for strength, and decorated with two carved lion and mock ring handles. *Courtesy of Penny Collection.* £150-200. $215-285

A slender octagonal tortoise shell bottle with indistinct engraved characters on one of its facets. *Courtesy of Penny Collection.* £80-100. $115-145

An unusual polished natural amber bottle with what appears to be a pair of lips carved into one side. The stopper is unusually large for the size of the bottle but is original. *Courtesy of Klemer Collection.* £80-100. $115-145

Simple in appearance, this amber bottle is complex in its construction having been made from over one hundred small blocks of natural amber assembled like a jigsaw and then polished to shape. £80-100. $115-145

A tiny carved cinnabar lacquer bottle decorated with images of bamboo, 1.25" (3 cm). *Courtesy of Penny Collection.* £120-150. $175-215

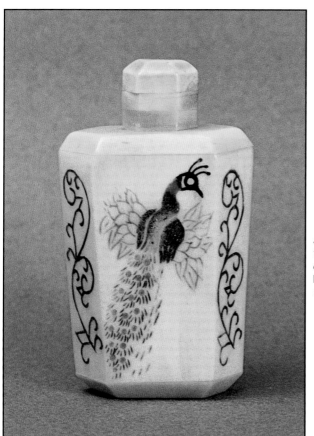

A six-sided composite bone bottle made from individual panels glued to form the overall shape. Each of the side panels has been engraved and painted. £60-80. $85-115

This double gourd shaped ivory bottle has a fine integral waist ring and tiny engraved and ink rubbed calligraphy. This reproduction of an old poem tells of a beautiful landscape where a hermit lives and wants to keep it to himself. The poet tells us that the hermit's body blends with the landscape. The characters also tell us the name of the carver which is *Xue Zhong Zi* and give a date in the Chinese lunar calender.
Courtesy of Klemer Collection.
£400-500. $575-715

A flattened vase shaped ivory bottle with finely engraved and colored detail. The picture of cranes is reinforced by the characters "*song he yang nian*" ("pine crane ongoing years") which is a wish for long life forever. Additional characters tell us that the painter of the original work which inspired this engraving was *Xia Cang Zi*. Additional small script reads "*qi shi qi shou Lu Shu Yi ke*" reading as "seventy-seven (year) old man (named) *Lu Shu Yi* carved". The quality and minute detail of the work on this bottle shows the experience but belies the age of the artist. *Courtesy of Klemer Collection.* £700-800. $1,000-1,145

A flattened ivory bottle deeply carved on both sides. Two boys play beneath a tree in a way which depicts celebration of the New Year, while on the reverse the character "fu" invokes good luck. Clearly this was intended as a New Year gift. *Courtesy of Klemer Collection.* £700-800. $1,000-1,145

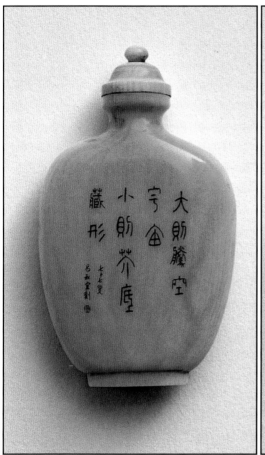 

This exquisite ivory bottle is finely engraved with an image of two dragons playing with or fighting over a flaming red pearl. A short poetic text decorates the back of the bottle with most of the engraving being highlighted by rubbed black ink. *Courtesy of Penny Collection.* £350-400. $500-575

This extraordinarily complex but tiny bottle is extremely delicate to handle. Carved in ivory this crab is fully articulated with the front pincers moving inwards to the prey which is the stopper. Dirty with age it would be a collector's nightmare to clean. *Courtesy of Penny Collection. £200-250. $285-360*

This tiny ivory bottle with an obvious Moorish influence has a screw-threaded stopper. The detail is excellent bearing in mind the size of the object being carved, 1.25" (3 cm). *Courtesy of Klemer Collection.* £120-150. $175-215

A small elegant ivory bottle with hunched shoulders and window panels which invite us into the lives of two mystics. £350-450. $500-645

Composite bone panelled bottle with four engraved and inked side panels. *Courtesy of Klemer Collection.* £40-50. $55-70

This very white ivory bottle is clearly fairly new and as such would be prevented from sale around most of the world. Few carvers now use ivory, most having turned their attention to other materials. This particular subject is a fish with a lotus flower stopper being captured by two boys who are too small to keep hold of it. They sit precariously on a bed of lotus buds, flowers, and pods. A small black speck features in an unfortunate place on the side of the fish but runs naturally through the entire depth of the bottle. *Courtesy of Aisingioro Collection. Photo by Ma Jun.* £500-600. $715-860

A finely carved ivory double gourd shaped bottle with tiny engraved detail and complex character structure by artist *Chen Ji Pin* now over eighty years old. The ability to engrave with a specific calligraphic style on this scale is very rare. *Courtesy of Aisingioro Collection.* £900-1,000. *Photo by Ma Jun.* $1,290-1,430

Chapter Eight
Inside Painted Snuff Bottles

In snuff bottle terms, the inside painted examples are relatively late arrivals and as such are ignored by many collectors. With a history barely exceeding a hundred years they came onto the scene at a time when actual snuffing or snuff taking was in decline but keen interest remained in the bottles as a collectors item.

Imperial interest in snuff bottles had already remained high for two hundred years with the quantity amassed in the Forbidden City running into tens of thousands. Because of this incredible focus on the Emperor and his followers it is reasonable to assume that as soon as inside painted bottles appeared they would have been presented to him.

The Forbidden City archives which recorded in great detail both the orders placed by the Emperors and the gifts given to them and their families record the first examples in the reign of Emperor Guangxu (1875-1908) during which around thirty artists became famous for their work and the craft reached its height. Two bottles with earlier reign marks for Qianlong (around 1810) in the Palace Museum Taipei (Taiwan) may be genuine but would beg the question about the lack of further development of the art for over half a century as no other examples are recorded. This new art form must have caused great delight to His Imperial Majesty who took such a keen interest in the subject and other examples soon followed.

Palace favorites were soon established resulting in several family dynasties of inside bottle painters being formed with techniques and styles being passed guardedly from father to son.

With the basic demise of the Imperial Household in 1912 much of the demand and impetus for the creativity in all forms of snuff bottles died. Despite this, fortunately, the art was passed down through the generations and several well known painting families today claim a continuous heritage back to the nineteenth century.

For the modern collector, it is usually the incredulity attached to inside bottle painting which hooks them in the first place.

There is no clear indication how inside painting came about but it is fairly safe to assume that it was out of need to keep the Emperor intrigued and happy.

It has been suggested to us by several of the most devoted Chinese collectors that whoever began the art must have been a Buddhist. At the time that would not have been especially unusual but the point they are making is that the sheer concentration and discipline required by the painter are beyond the comprehension of most people in the East or West but are typical of what might be expected of a Buddhist discipline.

The narrow hole traditional in snuff bottles does not lend itself to easy access for a paint brush, especially one loaded with paint, so apart from a slender finely tipped brush it also requires an extremely steady hand and a mind which can construct the painting in reverse. Simple bottles may be designed so that the artist creates an outline, usually in black, and then fills in the spaces created with colors. Complex subjects such as portraits or subtle landscapes require much more in the way of layering of the color and a real understanding of what will happen as the picture is built up in reverse from the first brush stroke.

There is no margin for error, of course, because each stroke is visible from the outside of the bottle and cannot easily be painted out or erased. While a few small strokes may be acceptable at the mouth of a cheap bottle, none can be countenanced at the mouth of an expensive one. Such errors may mean discarding a work that has taken days or even weeks to create.

There are many collectors in China and Taiwan today who seek out only modern bottles of high quality. Some have detailed knowledge of the artists and their previous work while the majority simply recognise a high quality piece of art and add it to their collections. Serious interest in the West is growing but the diehards still regard the modern bottles as "just for tourists". However, with prices reaching as high as £10, 000 for a new bottle that must surely rank as fine art and not tourist fodder.

The earliest examples in the nineteenth century generally followed traditional lines with delicate scenes of bridges, scholars, mountains and waterfalls and other subjects associated with Chinese symbolism. The majority of modern painters also follow these traditional designs, enhancing the images with poetic calligraphy, and often with a dedication to an earlier artist whose work they are immitating. This is much the same as one might see on an early European engraving or painting where the engraver or publisher refers to the picture as "after" the style of the original artist.

Seeking to enhance their standing some of the early painters also tackled portraiture, with exquisite results, providing some of the best portraits of late nineteenth and early twentieth century Imperial and high ranking family members which survive today.

Many of these are of photographic accuracy despite the fact that portraiture is one of the hardest subjects for the inside bottle painter to tackle. The subtlety of coloration and fine detail needed in order not to distort the features of the subject make these bottles highly prized. Watching an inside bottle painter at work for any length of time is fascinating but will almost certainly give the observer a headache. Few of us are accustomed to the level of concentration necessary.

The end of Imperial China and its subsequent years of upheaval, up to and after 1949, were not conducive to creativity of this kind and with the country almost completely closed to the West and generally languishing in poverty, there were few potential customers.

From 1949 onwards, however, with Mao Zedong at the helm, China looked towards many of its artisans for inspiration. Scholars were frequently ridiculed and their ideas suppressed but the artisans remained generally in favor. Hence, despite their connections with an Imperial past, there was a resurgence of interest in the skill or art of inside bottle painting. Mao himself approved the setting up of schools or academies for the redevelopment and expansion of the art. Many of the older painters whose work is revered today stem from this era and some of their early works reflect it with images of the propaganda and characters of revolution.

Several excellent portrait bottles exist of Mao Zedong as both revolutionary leader and later Chairman of the Communist Party and Head of State.

As with so many other aspects of snuff bottles, the variety of styles and designs are limited only by the imagination of the artist. A growing number of the better artists have expanded their range well beyond the traditional subjects but few have the skill to carry it off well. Western subjects emulating famous painters from *Van Gogh* to *Da Vinci* now attract high prices and are even being added to museum collections.

A collector in England recently commented of a bottle painted "after" the style of a *Botticelli* masterpiece that the original was exquisite, the inside bottle painted one was "awesome". Not only had it been miniaturized with such skill it was done with unenviable restrictions which *Botticelli* himself would not have contemplated.

The majority of good bottles will bear a small red signature or chop (seal) mark identifying the artist. These are often a simplified or stylized character of the artist's name but may also be little more than a squiggle in the same way that Western signatures on checks rarely resemble the writer's name. They usually indicate that the artist has graduated from one of the inside bottle painting Academies and is a painter of some note.

Of the good painters only a small percentage have achieved fame with collectors though many more should. Sadly most painters sell through agents who are not keen to promote one painter over another with the result that little information, other than perhaps a name, emerges for the collector.

When the subjects are Western and imitative they are rarely signed, the artists regarding it as an anomaly to have their chop mark on a Madonna and Child or landscape of thatched cottages. In collectors terms, this is of little consequence, the quality of the painting being paramount, but even without a signature it is often possible to recognize the work of a particular artist simply by style.

As mentioned earlier, a bottle we sold in 1999 for £400 changed hands three times in four days rising to £1,600 by the time it was sold to a collector who immediately recognized the hand of the painter he collected.

It is worth explaining that not all of these bottles are painted on the same material and that the creation of some bottles is almost as elaborate as their subsequent decoration.

A very small number of early and later bottles are made of natural rock crystal, agate or jade and have been polished to shape and then hollowed out to such an extent that the bottle is almost transparent. They can then be painted on the inside in the same way as glass. Such bottles are highly prized and can be very expensive.

Far more bottles are made of lead glass known in the West as crystal. These bottles are also created from a solid piece and are hollowed out, faceted and polished to the desired shape. They are generally quite heavy and the thick crystal glass of the sides creates effective magnifying and prismatic qualities which enhance the paintings. Such bottles tend to be better painted, as the initial materials are too expensive for the artists to produce shoddy work.

The hollowing of both of the above types of bottles creates a fairly coarse inner surface which is ideally suited to the inks used for painting. It allows them to adhere to the "frosted" surface in the same way as it might to paper or canvas.

The majority of cheaper tourist quality bottles are made of standard transparent glass blown into molds. These have little weight, can be cheaply bought by the painters and tend to have the amateur and student quality work within them. To create the desired surface for painting these bottles are treated to a wash of acid inside which slightly frosts the surface.

Two small blown glass bottles with complex street scenes backed with gold paint to enrich the image. £35-50 each. $50-70

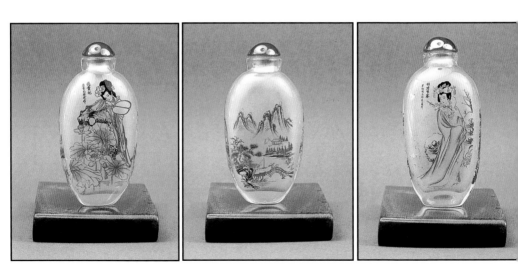

Three simple glass crystal bottles with monochrome painted interiors highlighted with a small amount of pink. Beautifully detailed work. £120-150 each. $175-215

A square sided glass crystal bottle painted with bright red blossom on plain black branches. Signed. £80-100. $115-145

Simplicity is the key in this signed squared glass crystal bottle showing delicate grasses in a dry landscape. £80-100. $115-145

Stems of freshly growing bamboo are a popular subject for Chinese artists of all kinds. Here the bamboo is simply depicted in mono-chrome inside this squared glass crystal bottle. Signed. £80-100. $115-145

A squared glass crystal bottle painted with chrysanthe-mum. Signed. £80-100. $115-145

Squared glass crystal bottle with simple black decoration of crabs with extensive poetic calligraphy. *Courtesy of Skippen Collection.* £60-80. $85-115

A simple glass crystal bottle with mountain and lake landscape. *Courtesy of Skippen Collection.* £50-60. $70-85

Brightly colored images of children playing feature on both sides of this blown glass bottle. *Courtesy of Skippen Collection.* £120-140. $175-200

An inexpensive student bottle depicting a man giving a speech. Unsigned. *Courtesy of Skippen Collection.* £30-40. $40-55

A colorful student bottle with a yellow background depicting the goddess *Guanyin*. Unsigned. *Courtesy of Skippen Collection*. £30-40. $40-55

A landscape and a lady leaning on a wall beneath blossoming trees decorate this fairly traditional advanced student bottle. *Courtesy of Skippen Collection*. £30-40. $40-55

Snow beautifully highlights both sides of this glass crystal bottle which features tigers. *Courtesy of Skippen Collection.* £140-160. $200-230

Two colorfully dressed ladies stand elegantly in the center of this thick-walled glass crystal bottle. The magnifying qualities of bottles of this kind make the paintings fascinating to examine from all angles. *Courtesy of Skippen Collection.* £100-120. $145-175

Elegant ladies in flowing Tang style costumes adorn these bottles. Each bottle has carved lion head and mock ring decorations and is carved in glass crystal. £120-150 each. $175-215

A carved glass crystal bottle with an image of the lady in a white trimmed red cloak on one side and ladies in Tang dress on the other. £150-180. $215-260

A heavy glass crystal faceted bottle painted with children playing "blind man's buff" and admiring a scroll. They are colorfully painted and have individual faces and expressions. £150-160. $215-230

An Imperial portrait and a section of the Great Wall decorate the two sides of this student bottle on sale to tourists. Even in China the buyer can expect to pay between £20 and £30 in an outdoor situation and as much as £60 in a hotel.

Opposite page,
Opposite page,
bottom: An attractive
glass crystal bottle is
topped with a nephrite
lion dog stopper above
elegant paintings of a
landscape with lakes
and pagodas.
Courtesy of Klemer
Collection. £200-
250. $285-360

A large inside painted table bottle showing a group of children (probably intended to be one hundred) celebrating the Dragon Festival. The quality of painting is not magnificent but it is nevertheless a vibrant and interesting bottle especially on this scale. The shape of the bottle, being very wide, makes it extremely difficult for the painter to reach the side areas with any degree of accuracy, 4.5" (11 cm) high, 5.0" wide (12.5 cm). £100-120. $145-175

A square clear glass bottle has been overlaid with red and then carved back to reveal four panels suitable for inside painting. The simple landscapes and calligraphy are typical of those of the nineteenth century. Wear on the bottle suggests that this is probably from that period. The poem contained in it was written by *Jai Dao* in the Tang dynasty, over one thousand years earlier. It tells the story of people visiting a mountain to find a wise man. They ask his pupils where he is but the pupils says he does not know because his master is inside the clouds picking herbs. The poems title is "*xun yin zhe bu yu*" ("going to find master not meet"). *Courtesy of Klemer Collection.* £250-300. $360-430

Opposite page, bottom: A heavy carved crystal bottle beautifully painted with tigers in a mountain landscape. Signed. £200-250. $285-360

A large inside painted glass crystal bottle with superb mountain landscape painting. Signed and with a poetic verse, 4.5" (11.5 cm). £200-250. $285-360

The interior of this large glass crystal bottle has been hollowed in a double gourd shape and is now the "canvas" for a complex painting depicting beautiful ladies from the Tang dynasty and young boys. *Courtesy of Skippen Collection.* £200-250. $285-360

A snowy landscape inspires a lone figure who overlooks it on one side of this bottle while a golden yellow background sets off monochrome detail of the mountain scene on the other. *Courtesy of Skippen Collection.* £160-180. $230-260

A series of waterfalls and the rocky landscape painted in brown and green decorate both sides of this glass crystal bottle. £150-180. $215-260

Four small animal and landscape subjects inside glass crystal bottles by artist *Hui Ran* (Mrs) who at the age of forty is now a well known and prize-winning painter. *Courtesy of Aisingioro Collection. Photo by Ma Jun.* £180-200 each. $260-285

A delicate lake scene with very subtle misty qualities by artist *Hui Ran* (Mrs). With painting of this quality her acclaim and prize-winning is no surprise. *Courtesy of Aisingioro Collection. Photo by Ma Jun.* £600-700. $860-1,000

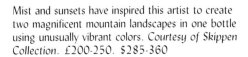

Mist and sunsets have inspired this artist to create two magnificent mountain landscapes in one bottle using unusually vibrant colors. *Courtesy of Skippen Collection.* £200-250. $285-360

Mountainous landscapes decorate both sides of this glass crystal bottle. Although not signed the workmanship of this painting is excellent. *Courtesy of Skippen Collection.* £180-200. $260-285

Scholars and their pupils or servants appear in this typically Chinese landscape featured inside a large glass crystal bottle. Signed, 4.5" (11 cm). *Courtesy of Skippen Collection.* £200-220. $285-315

The modern demand for well painted animal subjects is beautifully illustrated here in this glass crystal bottle depicting an elephant and a leopard. The superb quality of this artist's work is rarely matched. £250-300. $360-430

A twin glass crystal bottle with images of geese throughout the four seasons. Signed. £150-180. $215-260

The carved glass crystal bottle houses two pairs of beautifully painted monkeys in natural landscapes. £180-200. $260-285

Chinese year signs have formed the inspiration for this unusual bottle in blown glass. The use of black and white as a background is particularly striking. £160-180. $230-260

An ornately carved glass crystal bottle is the setting for these two European style landscapes which have a very three-dimensional quality. The artist has captured the essence of European water colorists as well as achieving the natural depth in such a landscape. As is typical of such subjects there is no Chinese signature. £250-300. $360-430

An unusually shaped faceted glass crystal bottle painted with fine detail of cranes standing in a rocky landscape. £250-300. $360-430

Opposite page: A superbly painted leopard resting in a tree forms one side of a naturalistic wildlife bottle. £250-300. $360-430

A misty mountain landscape at sunset occupies both sides of this large glass crystal bottle with double gourd shaped interior, 4.5" (11 cm). £200-250. $285-360

A pair of zebra in embrace and a doe and her fawn decorate the two sides of this glass crystal bottle symboliz-ing wishes for a long and happy marriage and the birth of a child. £140-160. $200-230

This large portrait bottle of the late Chairman *Mao Zedong* carries a potted history of his contribution to China on the reverse. Such portrait bottles are few and the ones created during the Cultural Revolution were obviously for propaganda purposes. This particular one was painted as a memorial and tells that he was born in 1893 and died eighty-three years later in 1976 having been Chairman of the People's Republic of China from 1949 to 1976. £100-150. $145-215

A magnificent African elephant stands ready to charge in this superb representation. The quality of the painting belies the limitations placed upon the painter, 4.5" (11 cm). £250-300. $360-430

A finely hollowed smokey quartz crystal bottle with simple monochrome internal decoration probably dating from the nineteenth century. *Courtesy of Klemer Collection.* £200-250. $285-360

A fine inside painted rock crystal snuff bottle by *Ye Zhongsan*, signed
Yi Si (corresponding to 1905), 68 mm. (A) £9,560. $13,670

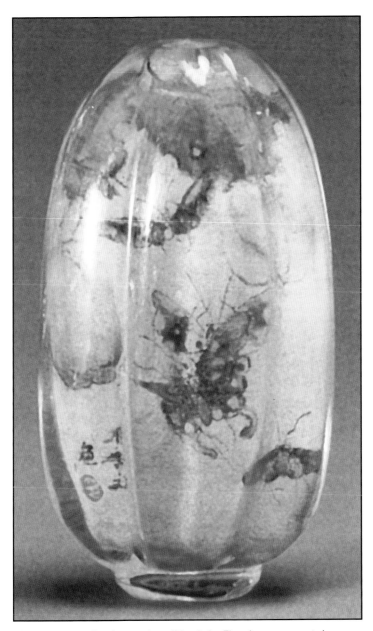

An inside painted rock crystal snuff bottle by *Zhou Leyuan*, twentieth century, 42 mm. (A) £2,400-3,200. $3,435-4,580

Chapter Nine
Fakes & Forgeries

In this category we must be quite clear what we are intending to highlight because definitions by other writers and collectors vary enormously.

As has already been mentioned it has been common practice for centuries in China to replicate the work of earlier craftsmen and often to replicate the marks and signatures that would be expected on such pieces. At the time this was done it was not for gain in the sense of deceiving buyers, as it might be today, but was considered a sign of great respect to a revered predecessor.

Similar practices today are referred to as forgery or faking. Earlier reference to the *Victoria & Albert* collection in London and its method of dating bottles shows that the only certainty was the date upon which a particular bottle was acquired. Such caution should still be exercised today unless extensive provenance can be proved.

In this chapter we are more concerned with materials that replicate the real ones and so may deceive the buyer irrespective of the claimed age of the item. With a wide range of resin based materials available today the list would be endless and yet the end products if not over priced can be an attractive addition for the collector on a modest budget.

With inside painted bottles in particular many incredulous observers and even occasionally supposed experts suggest that the feat they are observing is impossible and must have been achieved with a transfer. In fact the application of a transfer would be even more difficult than the painting which astounds them. A small number of tourist bottles, however, are being produced using a photographic technique. These are very poor in quality and should not deceive anyone.

Probably the most common of all the fakes are the creamy colored resins intended to look like ivory. Some have even got grain detail in them achieved by stretching the semi-cooled material to create streaks of color contrast. Other ivory look-alikes can also be found in bone but in this we need to be careful because bone was a material used in its own right for bottles of less importance. However, we will let the photographed examples tell their own story but it is clear from the illustrations that many are as attractive to look at and even handle as the ones they are imitating.

A molded pink resin is easily distinguished from the darker red cinnabar or heavier coral which it is trying to copy. Pretty as it may be this fake should not fool anyone but could still be included in a collection for its own sake. £20-25. $30-35

The basic material of this unusual-looking bottle caused considerable debate when it was first acquired. Its heavy weight and slightly streaky appearance to the brown body made glass a possibility but the black appeared to be onyx and the white ivory inlay, both of which would be highly unlikely in a glass bottle. The final test was a sharp blade to a small area of the foot which easily removed a small fragment of RESIN! This double-sided bottle has been very cleverly constructed and makes full use of the contrasting colors which have been inset with just as much skill as might have been used for more valuable materials. The subject of a tutor teaching a boy to read from a scroll is charming. Should this bottle be dismissed as a fake or accepted for what it is, a skilled piece of work in modern materials? £30-40. $40-55

Intended to look like either carved agate or amber, this bottle lacks the weight for the former but certainly has the color and the carving style. As an amber bottle it would be one of extraordinary quality with carved dark outer layers giving it an extremely attractive appearance. The fact that it is deliberately made in this way from resin should not totally detract from its collectibility since the faker's art is often worthy of recognition and in this case, the carver's art certainly is. £30-40. $40-55

Chapter Ten
Care & Display

Once you begin to develop a reasonable collection of bottles the matter of display can become a problem. It is tempting to keep them wrapped in cotton wool or in specially compartmentalized boxes but this defeats the object of their design which was to delight the senses and be admired.

Glass display cases, especially those with mirror backs and sides, are particularly suitable and the use of wooden or plastic stands will enhance them by varying the levels. Artificial lighting will help and can be added to an existing cabinet or incorporated into the design of one built for the purpose.

A collector friend recently sent a photograph of her pride and joy displayed neatly on glass shelves spanning her bathroom window. Her collection included both overlay glass and inside painted bottles. With the light from the window this may have seemed an ideal location but was far from it. From a purely practical point of view the repeated need to move the bottles for cleaning greatly increases the risk of damage from chipping. On a more serious note the strong light and heat from the window added to the dampness of the bathroom could quickly damage the inside painted bottles causing color to fade and possibly flake and even mould to develop if the stopper seals were not perfect. Some stone bottles such as turquoise, amethyst and coral would be equally unhappy in such a position as all suffer from strong light and heat.

If a collection includes ivory and bone bottles, or even wood, fruit stone or peel examples, then a small amount of humidity is advisable to avoid cracking. This can be achieved, in our over-heated Western homes, by placing a small bowl of water in the cabinet. This should not result in any condensation on the glass of the cabinet, but if it does the proximity of extreme heat or sunlight needs to be examined.

Whether your collection has cost thousands of pounds or not, it is yours and there to be enjoyed— so display it carefully and get the bottles out regularly to examine them and learn about them. It may also be fun to enhance the display with one or two old tins or containers of snuff, and perhaps some snuff saucers or bowls. Old Chinese photographs of people, who may well have been snuffers, can also enhance the scene and take the collector's imagination back to an age long gone.

Bibliography

Aisin-Gioro, Pu Yi. *From Emperor to Citizen: The Autobiography of Aisin-Gioro Pu Yi*. Beijing: Foreign Languages Press, 1989.

Keverne, Roger (Consultant Editor). *Jade*. London, New York: Anness Publishing Ltd., 1991.

Kleiner, Robert. *Chinese Snuff Bottles*. New York: Oxford University Press, 1994.

Li, He. *Chinese Ceramics: The New Standard Guide*. London: Thames and Hudson Ltd, 1996.

Perry, Lilla, S. *Chinese Snuff Bottles: The Adventures & Studies Of A Collector*. Rutland, Vermont and Tokyo: Charles E. Tuttle Company, Inc., 1960.

Rawson, Jessica (Editor). *The British Museum Book Of Chinese Art*. London: British Museum Press, 1992.

Stevens, Bob, C. *The Collector's Book Of Snuff Bottles*. New York: John Weatherhill, Inc., 1976.

White, Helen. *Snuff Bottles From China: The Victoria And Albert Museum Collection*. London: Bamboo Publishing Ltd., in association with the Victoria and Albert Museum, London, 1992.

Xia Gengqi, Zhang Rong, Chen Simin, and Luo Yang. *Masterpieces Of Snuff Bottles In The Palace Museum*. Beijing: Forbidden City Publishing House, 1995.